I0134425

Hadji in Syria

Also from Westphalia Press

westphaliapress.org

Hadji in Syria

or, Three Years in Jerusalem

by Sarah Barclay Johnson

WESTPHALIA PRESS
An imprint of Policy Studies Organization

Hadji in Syria, or, Three Years in Jerusalem
All Rights Reserved © 2016 by Policy Studies Organization

Westphalia Press
An imprint of Policy Studies Organization
1527 New Hampshire Ave., NW
Washington, D.C. 20036
info@ipsonet.org

ISBN-13: 978-1-63391-359-2
ISBN-10: 1-63391-359-7

Cover design by Taillefer Long at Illuminated Stories:
www.illuminatedstories.com

Daniel Gutierrez-Sandoval, Executive Director
PSO and Westphalia Press

Updated material and comments on this edition
can be found at the Westphalia Press website:
www.westphaliapress.org

HADJI IN SYRIA;

OR,

Three Years in Jerusalem.

BY

MRS. SARAH BARCLAY JOHNSON.

PHILADELPHIA:

JAMES CHALLEN & SONS.

J. B. LIPPINCOTT & CO., Nos. 22 & 24 NORTH FOURTH ST.

LONDON: TRÜBNER & CO.

1858.

GROUP IN THE BAZAARS.

PUBLISHERS' PREFACE.

A FEW explanatory remarks would seem to be appropriate with reference to this little "messenger from a strange land," on making its Salaam to the Public.

The Authoress, deeming that but few of the incidents she had journalized during her residence in Palestine would be sufficiently interesting to justify their publication, declined every solicitation to furnish them for the press—knowing how well the public have already been supplied with works on the Holy Land. But we confidently believe that the public will be satisfied with the judgment which her friends have passed upon the work, in overcoming her scruples on this point.

A hiatus was believed to exist which it is deemed desirable to supply—and being assured that amongst all the varied productions on this fruitful subject, with which this country has been favoured, this one will find its appropriate place; the publishers have spared no pains in giving it a suitable dress in which to appear before the reading world.

All the illustrations being selected from her own portfolio, their correctness may be implicitly relied upon; and thus a more correct idea of the matters portrayed may be derived from their inspection, than from the most extended verbal description.

CONTENTS.

LIST OF ILLUSTRATIONS.

ENGRAVED BY LOUDERBACK & HOFFMAN, FROM DESIGNS BY WHITE & PERKINS.

HADJI IN SYRIA.

CHAPTER I.

LAND HO! LAND!!

SUCH was the joyful exclamation of the man on the mast-head, as he caught the first glimpse of a hazy streak in the distant horizon. "Land!" And such land as it was, too! not only terra firma, but "Terra Santa." The land of patriarchs and prophets—the land of apostles, martyrs, and confessors—the Land of Emmanuel! the Holy Land!

Adventurous, chivalrous, and romance-loving Palmers of every age and clime have preceded us in this pilgrimage; but few, perhaps, have hailed this haven with purer delight than that which now glowed in our bosoms.

The emotions with which the wearied pilgrim voyager hails the first glimpse of "Canaan's happy shore," after encountering the perils of two mighty seas, are surely akin to those experienced by the disembodied spirit on entering the haven of the Canaan above, after voyaging in life's frail bark over the tempestuous ocean of time.

A succession of frightful storms having well-nigh destroyed our noble barque, we had left it at Malta, and taken passage on board the screw steamer "Brigand." And intensely were we longing to descry in the distance the dim blue line that none but an experienced voyager would suspect of being other than a cloud. Day after day was a brave and active "tar" sent to the top of the mast, with the hope of hearing the longed-for sound of "Land ho!" At last the cry was heard—a little while, and we ourselves succeed in piercing the mists that for a time baffle all our efforts at getting a glimpse of the shore. Soon trees and houses appear, and then the moving people.

The ponderous anchor is gradually prepared for a launch—a loud splash and clatter, and we are safely anchored, no longer the sport of howling winds and angry seas. And the dropping of the anchor is by no means an unimportant event in a traveller's experience—not unlike the falling of the chains from a convict on his release from the gloomy walls of his prison. For have we not been held in "durance vile" for weeks and months within our little cell-like cabin, exercising all the hopes and fears that agitate the breast of the prisoner on shore— now cheered by a faint gleam of sunshine, and now waiting in the breathless silence of fear to be engulfed by mountain waves.

But it was not without some regret that we bade adieu to the great deep over which we had passed; and, while longing to set foot on holy land, I could but meditate upon its vastness and majestic flow, and give expression to my thoughts in Byron's beautiful apostrophe :—

> " Roll on, thou deep and dark blue ocean—roll !
> Ten thousand fleets sweep over thee in vain ;
> Man marks the earth with ruin—his control
> Stops with the shore ; upon the watery plain
> The wrecks are all thy deed, nor doth remain
> A shadow of man's ravage, save his own,
> When, for a moment, like a drop of rain,
> He sinks into thy depths with bubbling groan,
> Without a grave, unknelled, uncoffined, and unknown.

> " Thy shores are empires, changed in all save thee ;
> Assyria, Greece, Rome, Carthage, what are they ?
> Thy waters wasted them while they were free,
> And many a tyrant since ; their shores obey
> The stranger, slave, or savage ; their decay
> Has dried up realms to deserts ; not so thou,
> Unchangeable save to thy wild waves' play—
> Time writes no wrinkle on thy azure brow—
> Such as creation's dawn beheld, thou rollest now."

Who would fail to gaze in admiration at the lovely landscape spread before us ! The snowy peaks of Lebanon, " that goodly mountain," are in full view : the deep blue Mediterranean is spotted here and there with sails of dazzling white, and scarcely less white are the terraced houses of Beirût, bathed in bright oriental sunshine, and viewed through the clear ethereal atmosphere peculiar to this classic and biblical clime.

Beirût is one of the prettiest of eastern towns, and just now has donned her gayest attire—this being the hour when the inhabitants, in their picturesque costumes, are grouped upon every house-top, to enjoy the twilight hour and the glory of the setting sun.

Lodgings are secured at " La Bellevue" hotel, a half oriental, half European establishment, very popular withal from its beautiful situation on the seashore. Following the example of our neighbors, we resort to the roof of the house, whence we can the better feast our eyes on the novel scene. Everything reminds us that we are in the land of the Bible, and our first impulse leads us to take the holy record in hand; and while turning from one graphic

2

description to another, we lift our eyes from the page to gaze upon the reality.

Looking down into the court, two women are seen grinding wheat, with just such a mill as that to which our Saviour referred in his prophetic denunciation: "Two women shall be grinding at the mill, the one shall be taken, the other left." It consists of two circular stones, the upper one having a handle, by which both the women rapidly whirl the stone round and round upon the lower one, which is immovable. This is often accompanied by singing, which, together with the noise made by the grinding, explains the passage in Jeremiah, where the Almighty declares He will take away from the Jews

"The voice of mirth, and the voice of gladness,
The voice of the bridegroom, and the voice of the bride,
The sound of the *mill-stone*, and the light of the candle,
And the whole land shall be a desolation and an astonishment."

The strangest of sights and sounds arrest our attention! But what fragmentary checkered

pavement is this on which we are walking—
white, black, reddish, and bluish little cubes of
marble? It is the floor of an old Roman man-
sion. But, alas! what a change has come over
this ancient seat of lore and chivalry—the
world-famed capital of the famous colony of
Julia Felix! Where are the covenant Hebrews
that once dwelt here? Where the proud Ro-
mans that vanquished and enslaved them?
Where the Persians, Greeks, Saracens, crusaders, and hosts of its other captors? All have
given way to the Ottoman Turk, "the worst of
the heathen." But what are these that slowly
approach us in the habiliments of the grave?
Are they spectres or very ghosts? A nearer
approach reveals the fact, however improbable
in the distance, that they belong to the category of my own sex—booted and pantalooned
though they be! One shudders at their sepulchral appearance, completely enveloped as they
are in those white sheets. And who are these
in long gowns, gaudy sashes, morocco slippers,

and beautiful tiaras? Well, these turn out
to be the rulers of the land—"the turbaned
Turk."

What motley groups crowd the streets—
quadrupeds as well as bipeds! Surly Turks,
stolid Arabs, hardy Druses, wily Maronites,
travellers from the ends of the earth, and here
and there a poor despised Jew—the rightful
owner of the land. What jargon in the
bazaars! a very Babel! Who can help laugh-
ing outright to see the Frank mounted on that
little donkey, with his legs bent at right angles
to keep his feet above ground; and the poor
woman astride on the mule—but we will soon
be accustomed to the sight. Fine Arab steeds
are prancing about, impatient of restraint; and
there goes a fleet of five-and-twenty heavily-
freighted "ships of the desert," piloted by one
little donkey, going down the coast of Phœnicia.
There goes an Arab porter trudging along with
a veritable barrel of American flour on his back.
What admirable beasts of burden are these

domesticated wild men of the desert—the pos-
terity of Ishmael!

Of the ten thousand words I have heard from
these various tribes, not one syllable have I
understood.   Be not surprised, then, that when
I heard a child cry in real good English, I could
but feel a momentary satisfaction in being reminded of my country by this imp of Mohammed,
so lustily expressing his sentiments in the very
language used by the little urchins of America!
Still more satisfactory was it to find the canine
citizens giving expression to their views and
feelings of matters and things in the same
classic *lingo* that distinguishes the "friend of
man" in occidental climes!

The most singular fancy that one meets
with, is the head-dress of the Druse women,
which is assumed at the nuptial ceremony—
never more to be laid aside.   A long silver
horn projects from the forehead, over which a
white veil is hung, nearly covering her person.
This is certainly a more comfortable way of

2 *

concealing the face, than the closely drawn
veil of the Turkish lady, inasmuch as the horn
gives room for a free circulation of air. To
the base of this heavy fixture, a quantity of
silver balls, silk tassels, and other trinkets, are
hung. The horn is about two feet in length,
and is never even temporarily removed, being
fastened to a cushion, which is tightly tied to
the head. The sight of this strange head-gear
forcibly brings to mind several passages of
Scripture, showing its ancient origin :—1 Sam.
ii. 1, " And Hannah prayed and said, My heart
rejoiceth in the Lord, mine horn is exalted in
the Lord." Psalm lxxxix. 24, " And in my
name shall his horn be exalted." In another,
" I said to the wicked, Lift not up the horn ;"
and again, " And in thy favor our horn shall
be exalted." And Job says, " I have defiled
mine horn in the dust." These (one is strongly
inclined to believe) referred to the same ornament, probably in use among the daughters of
Shem. One can't help believing they must be

heartily tired of the state of single life, to assume this inconvenient burden, in addition to the thousand and one cares and anxieties that go to make up the sum and substance of connubial bliss among oriental females; it is highly gratifying to learn, however, that the missionaries in Beirût and Mount Lebanon are doing, and indeed have done, much to ameliorate the moral, mental, and physical condition of this strange class of people, who originated in the following manner :—

After the death of Mohammed, many disputes arose amongst his followers, causing great dissension, and ultimately giving rise to many sects and creeds. History records no less than sixty, each having a leader or an apostle, who zealously disseminated his own peculiar doctrines. At this time a ruler arose amongst them whose career was one of madness and folly. Among his extravagant actions, we read that he compelled all Jews and Christians, among whom he had power, to renounce their

religion and adopt his own. Such was his
hatred for Mohammed, that he ordered his
khalifs to be publicly cursed in the mosques,
and prohibited the pilgrimage to Mecca, as well
as fasting and the five Mohammedan prayers.

Wishing one day to indulge in a piece of innocent sport, he caused the half of Cairo to be
burnt, and the remaining half to be plundered!
At another time, he caused an entire cessation
in the manufacture of women's slippers, which
he considered an indispensable precautionary
measure to compel the women to remain within
doors.

He had sixteen thousand followers, and a
close friend in the person of Mohamed-ben-Is-
rael, whom he styled his prophet. This prophet was taken into especial favor because he
acknowledged his master to be God himself—
but not so with the people. They frowned
upon his madness, and finally assassinated both
ruler and prophet. This rash act, however,
had not the desired effect of checking the pro-

gress of their opinions. A large society was formed, taking the name of Druses, from El Dorzi, the first and most zealous preacher who continued to disseminate the doctrines of their massacred ruler. These strange people have since undergone many changes. At the beginning of the seventeenth century, they obtained great power under their talented leader, Faker-el-din or Fakardin, who, after a most eventful life, was strangled A. D. 1631, by order of the Sultan.

The Druses are now living quietly, and have for their capital a town of about five thousand inhabitants; their number throughout the country being two hundred thousand. Travellers tell us that they lead a very simple life. The palace of their chief or Emir, however, is said to be very elegant, having marble floors and splendid tapestries. Among their peculiarities, they do not condemn marriage between brothers and sisters; and, unlike the Mohammedans, allow the consumption of pork and wine.

As for their religious ceremonies, nothing
can be said of them, for their greatest care is
to meet together in secrecy, and thus involve
their form of worship in mystery. It is known,
however, that the greater part of the nation
deny the doctrine of a future state.

The Maronites, some of whom are also to be
seen in Beirût, took their name from their prophet Maron, who was held by them in such
veneration, that they affirm miracles to have
been wrought in virtue of his remains. They
are divided into two classes, the sheikhs and the
common people, who are very hospitable, keeping open houses for the entertainment of
strangers. They condemn a plurality of wives,
and in religious matters principally hold the
doctrines of Rome. This is said to be the only
sect which is allowed to have bells to all their
chapels—a privilege which, though generally
denied other churches throughout the Turkish
dominions, is yet tolerated in most of the convents; and in some of them a suspended bar of

wood is made to subserve the purposes of a bell.

But interesting as the city of Berytus unquestionably is, there are localities further on far more so; and now we begin to think of taking up our line of pilgrimage.

Joseph, the hero of Mr. Brown's admirable "Yuseph," with his huge bundle of letters of recommendation, presents himself, with the assurance that he will be the most faithful of dragomans, should we be pleased to engage his services. A glance at his bristling girdle suffices to elicit from us a favorable answer. It is overflowingly supplied with dirks, sabres, and pistols; accoutrements to which no one, in anticipation of a passage through a wild region of country, alleges the slightest objection. Thus equipped, and mounted on his fiery Arabian steed, we deem him a match for half a dozen Bedawin: a most consoling thought, in view of the double capacity in which he is about to act, as guard and dragoman to Jeru-

salem. He wears the usual gay costume of
the Greek Arabs. A tarbouch of bright crimson, a jacket of purple, richly embroidered with
gold, a vest of delicate green embroidered with
silks, a white plaited skirt, twenty yards wide,
and boots of bright yellow morocco, complete
his attire.

With an unmistakeable air of self-import-
ance, he takes upon himself the command of
our cavalcade, on starting for Jerusalem. To
hear the deafening tones in which he gives
orders and directions to the awe-inspired mule-
teers, you would conceive him to be the Pacha
himself—a conception not altogether foreign to
his own mind! His accomplishments are varied as the contents of his girdle: there is no
better cook to be found in the land; no one
can place a lady on her horse with more grace
and gallantry; and the country does not produce a greater linguist, speaking fluently, as
he does, no less than six or seven languages.
Bravery is another attribute for which he is

equally renowned. The most wonderful accounts of his daring exploits with the marauding Bedawin, are told far and near; whether true or not is hard to tell, in this heaven-abandoned land, where truth is so lightly esteemed and rare.

JEWISH QUARTER SHEKEL.

CHAPTER II.

FROM BEIRUT TO JERUSALEM.

"It is a goodly sight to see
What Heaven hath done for this delicious land!
What fruits of fragrance blush on every tree!
What goodly prospects o'er the hills expand!
But man would mar them with an impious hand."

WITH bounding spirits, and hopeful happy hearts, we at last form the line of march, and enter upon our journey, every preparation having been made—horse, foot, and dragoon— tent and canteen—goods and chattels, and all the thousand and one items that Syrian travel renders necessary for comfort and safety—the entire cavalcade being led by a donkey but little larger than a Newfoundland dog.

We take the seacoast route along the once crowded track of Phœnician commerce: but, alas! how desolate is the present appearance of the country, lying as it now does, under the curse of Heaven!

We must stop an hour at noon and lunch in a roadside khan, where we are but poorly sheltered from the pattering rain which is falling in torrents. These stopping-places are but little better than the most ordinary stables in our own favored country, being nothing more than a stone house, or mud hut, with earthen floors, bare walls, and unglazed windows. Such is our present little caravanserai,—but Yuseph promises us a night's lodging in the best khan in all Syria. We, therefore, halt at the door of the celebrated " Nebi-Yunas khan" (khan of the Prophet Jonas), in anxious expectation of being fully repaid for the fatigue of our day's journey by the comforts and luxuries very naturally suggested by Yuseph's promise. But, shade of Jonas! what is our surprise, on entering a room with floor uncovered either by carpet or matting, without table, chair, or divan—*sans*

everything—presenting, in the absence of a
single piece of furniture, anything but the air
of comfort we had been led to anticipate. It
is but sheer justice, however, to state that
although the door was no sufficient barrier
even against the prowling jackals that were
howling about, yet the windows were windows
that were *wind-doors*, admitting light, wind,
and birds, without let or hindrance. But what
care we for table or chair? Hunger and a
long ride in the drenching rain suggest other
things, with which we resolve to be content.
Our wants, if not our anticipations, are fully
met in a pan of hot coals, and a frugal supper
furnished from the mysteries of the "canteen"
—an indispensable item of our caravan furniture, inasmuch as it contains our provisions,
and constitutes our locomotive kitchen. The
daughters of the land come in, and, in order to
have some pretext for extorting from us the
bucksheesh of a few piastres, dance before us
with all their might, our earnest entreaties to

the contrary notwithstanding. Mats and pieces of baggage are now substituted for beds, and fatigue secures for us that deep and refreshing repose so little known to the pampered epicure.

At early dawn we rise to resume our journey, quite as willing, perhaps, to leave our Arab khan as Jonah was to quit his fishy lodging— for it is here, as the monks will have it, that the timid prophet was disembarked from aboard the submarine whaler! Our ride is now along the coast of Phœnicia—the great line of trade and travel in days of yore. Sidon, the city of prophecy, is reached about midday, and, soon after our entrance, we receive an official call from Ibrahim Nukley, the polite and obliging consular representative of the "stars and stripes." He inquires very earnestly after the welfare of our great American statesman, " *Sultan* Cass," as he called him, who, some time since, made a tour to the Holy Land, and impressed the people very favorably.

The palaces of the merchant princes that
3 *

once adorned the streets of Sidon have long since been levelled to the dust, and her territory despoiled by the Persian hordes that invaded this ground in direct fulfilment of prophecy. There is nothing now to be seen of this sin-smitten city but a few fragments of columns or archways, and other ruins lying here and there in confused heaps. What a striking instance of the visitation of Jehovah's wrath is the downfall of this city that was called, in the day of her power, the "mother of commerce!" Among the most fearful of the threats against Sidon is the following, recorded by Ezekiel: "Thus saith the Lord; behold, I am against thee, O Zidon; and I will be glorified in the midst of thee: and they shall know that I am the Lord, when I shall be sanctified in her." Thus we now behold only a miserable little Arab village, a few scattered ruins of former grandeur, and a single schooner riding at anchor in the harbor, as representatives of the navy and city of Sidon. Luxuriant bananas,

and other semi-tropical fruits, abundantly testify in behalf of this productive soil and genial
clime—" A delightsome land, saith the Lord of
Hosts!"—" The glory of all lands."

Having fully surveyed the doomed city, we
again take up the line of march, and soon call
a halt at a picturesque fountain on the roadside, where we are honored with the company
of a Turkish dignitary.   Some of these fountain structures, that are used as oratories, are
in very good preservation, and convey a good
idea of Saracenic architecture.   Reluctantly
leaving this sweet place of repose, in due time
we reach Tyre, the next point of interest, another devoted city of prophecy; of which it is
said, " Thou art situate at the entry of the sea
—a merchant of the people for many isles."
" The ships of Tarshish did sing of thee in
thy market." " Thou wast perfect in thy ways
until iniquity was found in thee."   Of the rig-
ging of her ships it is said, " Fine linen, and
broidered work from Egypt, was that which

thou spreadest forth to be thy sail;" and of
her beauty, "Thou hast said I am of perfect
beauty;" but, because of her sins, "She was
cast, as profane, out of the mountain of God."
So signally has she fallen from the pinnacle of
her glory, down to the nadir of desolation, that
not a vestige now remains of her former mag-
nificence. How wonderful in our eyes is the
fulfilment of the most minute prediction uttered
against these ill-fated cities of the East!

It was predicted of Tyre, "I will make thee
like the top of a rock. Thou shalt be a place
to spread nets upon, for I, the Lord, have
spoken it, saith the Lord." Accordingly, the
first objects that attract the attention of the
traveller are fishermen's nets spread on the
rocks! Her destitute appearance extorts the
involuntary exclamation, "How art thou destroyed that wast inhabited of seafaring men—
the renowned city which was strong in the
sea!" "Is this your joyous city, whose antiquity was of ancient days?"

Here was the capital of Hiram, who supplied Solomon with the cedars of Lebanon for the building of the "House of the forest of Lebanon," and for navies and ships of trade as well as for the magnificent temple. Tyre did not always continue in her fallen state, for it was written, "And it shall come to pass in that day that Tyre shall be forgotten seventy years, according to the years of one king." After the lapse of these seventy years she once more became the "crowning city," and continued the occupation of trading until the destructive siege of Alexander, foretold by Ezekiel in these significant words, "They shall lay thy stones, and thy timber, and thy dust, in the midst of the water." From this time the sceptre passed away from her for ever.

The American consular agent lost no time in calling upon us, and, like the dignified functionary of Sidon, tendered the hospitalities of his mural domicil (for it is built upon the wall); but we preferred the freedom of our

hired lodgings—no mean establishment either
—for amongst other luxuries we had silk cover-
lets. The floor was our bedstead, however,
and the beds simply a little cotton or wool
sewed up in a flat bag of sufficient dimensions
for the accommodation of one person. These
are all piled up the one on the other during
the day, and at night each person goes to the
general magazine and bears off his bed when
and where he lists. This, however, is the bed
of the upper circles. That of the common
people is still more portable, and easily arranged, being made simply by lying down!
for the plebeian carries on his back throughout
the day "that whereon he lieth" at night; and
thrice happy is the Arab who, in addition to
this large outer garment, can boast of a piece
of matting which he can interpose between
himself and the ground by way of mattress.

The consul's wife accompanied her lord, and
was evidently pleased at the glances of wonder we bestowed on the lavish display of gold

and jewels covering her head and shoulders; her enormous head-dress hanging quite to her girdle. She placed it on my head, but I could scarcely hold myself erect a single minute; and well may it be so weighty, for it contained several thousand dollars worth of jewels, besides numberless gold and silver coins, pierced and strung on her long hair, which hung, veil-like, over her back in a profusion of little braids. Did she but possess the inner "ornament of a meek and quiet spirit" at all proportionate to her outer adornment, she would certainly never disturb the quietude of the consulate.

But few remains of Tyre can now be discerned among the miserable collection of fishing-huts, called by the Arabs "Sour." In a walk along the beach, we gather some of the beautiful shells from which the alchemists of yore are supposed to have extracted the celebrated Tyrian purple.

Leaving Tyre, we journey towards St. Jean

d'Acre, the Akko of the Old Testament, and the Ptolemais of the New, which can boast of nothing more than its formidable-looking walls, the houses being a mass of patched-up ruins,— and the streets narrow and filthy. Its unprepossessing appearance does not tempt us to tarry longer within its walls than suffices to refresh our wearied bodies; so, cheerfully returning the salaam of the soldiers who guard its gate, we enter the plain of Esdraelon, celebrated as the battle-ground of nations; and a most unfortunate one it was for the great soldier of France, whose ambitious designs here received a check from which *le grand Empereur* never recovered. This part of the country, and indeed nearly the whole of the ground over which we have passed, is carpeted with flowers of endless variety, far more brilliant, in color and greater in size than the wild flowers of our own land. I can no longer suspect a lady traveller in this land, of exaggeration, who speaks of having collected a hundred distinctly different flowers during a short walk.

Several of our most spirited horses having engaged in a terrible fight, and one of them being seriously injured, we are fearful of delay. The proud steed struggles with what may prove a fatal wound. But in an instant, Yuseph puts spurs, or rather shovels (for such they are), to his spirited horse, and flying away to a copse of shrubs, speedily returns with a handful of leaves, which he reduces to a pulp, and applies to the gaping wound. The blood is staunched almost immediately, and now we resume our journey, and are on the *qui vive* for adventure or anything of interest.

> "Hark, a sound in the valley! where swollen and strong,
> Thy river, O Kishon, is sweeping along;
> Where the Canaanite strove with Jehovah in vain,
> And thy torrent grew dark with the blood of the slain."

Further on, we ford the deep and rapid current of "that ancient river, the river Kishon,"

4

whose waters were once crimsoned with the
blood of four hundred false teachers, slain at
the command of the prophet of God.   It was
on this very plain, too, that Deborah, that
good old mother in Israel, achieved such a
splendid victory over Sisera, the commander
of the army of Jabin, king of Canaan.   And
here also was performed that courageous act of
another daring woman, which is thus com-
mended by the sacred writer : " Blessed among
women shall Jael the wife of Heber the Ke-
nite be."

A well known traveller says he never saw
the process of pitching a tent without bringing
to mind the story of Jael and Sisera.   To this
day the " nail and hammer" compose an important part of household furniture.   In the
erection of a tent these are indispensable.   The
" nails" consist generally of mere wooden pegs,
to which the cords of the tent are fastened.
These are again alluded to in one of the pro-
phecies relating to Jerusalem : " Thine eyes

shall see Jerusalem a quiet habitation, a taber-
nacle that shall not be taken down; not one
of the stakes thereof shall ever be removed,
neither shall any of the cords thereof be
broken."

The tents commonly used are gayly colored
and highly ornamental; but those in which the
Bedawin encamp are black, the material being
the skins of black goats. We are thus enabled
to understand the following portion of Solomon's Song: "I am black but comely, oh ye
daughters of Jerusalem, as the tents of Kedar,
as the curtains of Solomon." Some of these
black tents are now to be seen in the distance,
and vividly recall the passage.

The steep ascent of Mount Carmel is now
commenced on foot. Our road is nothing more
than a series of little holes worn in the rock
by the beasts of burden that constantly climb
the "ladder," laden with fruits and merchan-
dise. Our path is often on the edge of a preci-
pice, several hundred feet in height, almost

overhanging the sea, and a single misstep would hurl us below into the surging ocean.

Our horses with the greatest possible difficulty, but with studied *care*, pursue the toilsome ascent, and were they any other than oriental horses, would stumble and fall at every step. Fortunate indeed are we that they are trained to this mode of travelling! These dangerous passes no doubt suggested the figure found in several passages of Scripture, which would not forcibly strike the mind of those inhabiting a more level country. David prays that his "enemies may not rejoice over him when his foot slippeth." Of the wicked, God says, "To me belongeth vengeance and recompense; their foot shall slide in due time." How significant is this figure to those travelling over these lofty summits, and along the verge of these frightful precipices!

Situated on the top of the mountain is the neat and elegant Convent of Elijah, affording delightful entertainment for the wearied Hadji,

not a little enhanced by its extensive view of
the surrounding country. Its monastic occupants are said to lead a most rigorous and
secluded life, wearing no sandals, and abstain-
ing from meat. A chapel is shown, and under
its altar a grotto, said to have been one of the
homes of Elijah. This, however, is one of
many caves with which the mountain abounds;
any one of which, we have just as great reason
to select as the Tishbite's abode, as that pointed
out by tradition. Was it not to these very caves
that Amos referred when speaking of the
attempts of the wicked to escape their inevitable doom, in these words: "Though they hide
themselves in the top of Carmel, Jehovah will
search and take them out thence"? Notwithstanding the long neglect of this region, the
soil is still very fertile, and agrees well with
the account of Isaiah, who speaks in such glowing terms of the "excellency of Carmel." A
celebrated naturalist found here forty-seven
varieties of flowers, and says that a botanist

4 *

might spend a year in this delightful retreat,
and every day add new specimens to his collection.

After a few hours' recreation we very cor-
dially exchanged salaams and bucksheeshes
with the warm-hearted "Padre Charley," who
very kindly presented me with a vial of fragrant essence, and reluctantly bid adieu to this
delightful spot, so rich in its soul-stirring remi-
niscences and associations.   Descending the
mountain, we resume our line of march along
the seashore—often, indeed, making a little
marine excursion amongst the waves that gently
lave the sandy beach.

Never did band of "hadjis" more joyously
wend their way over "Terra Santa," than did
our happy company of palmers on this occasion.
But here it behoves me, as a faithful journalist,
to record how low my pride was brought in a
single moment of misfortune, as we were passing the ruins of Ahtlit—exemplifying in one
sense at least the declaration that "pride goeth

before destruction, and a haughty spirit before a fall." The beautiful trim filly with which I was provided, had often contested in races it would seem, as every well-favored horse in that country is bound to do. She was thought to be too fiery for me on commencing our journey; but, inasmuch as she was led by a steady muleteer, it was deemed prudent to confide me to her back. But pluming myself not a little upon my rare equestrian tact, I ventured to dismiss the muleteer after a day's travel, supposing that I had gained the *mastery* over her proud spirit. Queen Dido herself in her girlish days perhaps never sat more elate with self-satisfaction upon her saddle (if saddle they had in those days!), as she rode up and down this very shore, than did your self-confident Hadji as she rode past the ruins of Ahtlit. But alas for budding pride! Yuseph, who had lingered behind for some time, came flying past me on his elegant sorrel charger, and in a moment my ambitious filly, regarding it as a

challenge, gave one snort of defiance, and was
off like the lightning! But poor me! Reader,
what do you think became of the proud equestrian Hadji! There I lay half buried in the
sand and shells, and all my proud aspirations
of equestrian celebrity with me. The reader
will not, therefore, be surprised when I confess
that everything like pride of horsemanship I
have since eschewed and left behind me en-
tombed in the sands of Ahtlit!—concluding
that " an horse is a vain thing for safety."

In disagreeable contrast with the luxuries
of the convent, is our night's lodging at the
filthy little mud village of Tantura, where we
are compelled to spend the night. Here we lie
on the bare ground, in the same room—if such
I may call the mud wall and bush-top pen in
which we lodged—with all kinds of animals,
not excepting several species of the insect tribe;
and these, though the most diminutive in size,
cause us the greatest amount of trouble. One
could patiently endure the company of such

harmless companions as the horses, mules, donkeys, cows, cats, and rats, that jointly occupied the room with us; but that of the smaller order interferes most materially both with one's bodily rest and equanimity of mind. Never did we leave a place with such heart-felt joy; never was breakfast so hastily despatched, and preparations completed in so short a space of time as those preceding our departure next morning. But apropos of this same "*oriental* insect," as it is called,—there is a certain plant growing abundantly hereabouts, as we afterwards learned, which instantly paralyzes these nimble-footed gentry. A portion of the powdered leaf not exceeding a pin's head in size, if placed in their vicinity, will instantly prove fatal—as I have often seen proved by the natives for the conviction and amusement of curious and incredulous travellers.

We shortly come in sight of Cæsarea. It was here that Paul spoke so eloquently before Felix, Agrippa, and the beautiful but ill-famed

Bernice; here the Gentiles were first received into the church, and here too Herod Agrippa "was smitten by the angel, and consumed of worms, because he gave not God the glory." This famous city was also the dwelling-place of Philip the Evangelist, and his "five virgin daughters who did prophesy." Although once so important, Cæsarea is now merely marked by magnificent ruins; and its only inhabitants are howling jackals and unapproachable porcupines, the dancing satyrs of Scripture; bringing to mind the following prediction, now so literally verified: "Their towers and fortresses shall become dens for wild beasts."

Here Yuseph has an opportunity of displaying his valor, for we are suddenly startled by the appearance of wild Bedawin, dimly seen within the mouth of a dark cave. Yuseph, however, is accustomed to these things, for he tells us "he has kilt more than one of these fellows in his day." With a grand flourish of the deadly instruments carried in his girdle, he soon frightens them off, much to the joy of all our company, but is evidently no little frightened himself, as well he might be, at the thought of such unequal combat—for their numbers far exceeded ours, and the wonder is they did not put their evidently preconcerted scheme into effect.

And this is not the only adventure which signalized our ride through this wild region of country. On arriving at the banks of a deep and rapid river farther on, Yuseph himself hesitated to attempt a passage. All agreed that such a thing was preposterous, and the ladies of course endorsed this fully. One of the party was despatched higher up the stream, in the hope of finding a safer crossing-place; and as he drew near on his return, I anxiously scrutinized his brown face, in search of kindling eye and joyous countenance—sure indications of good news; but good news he had none; on the contrary, a passage was less feasible higher up than where we stood. A party of Bedawin

approached, and for the first time we felt a
sense of relief instead of fear, at the sight of
their dark forms, for we thought perchance
their familiarity with the country might afford
us some assistance in finding a crossing-place.
Sure enough they were quite ready to pilot us
across, but insisted upon the safety of crossing
at that very spot.   One of them waded far into
the stream, and beckoned us to follow.   Fear-
lessly we now urged our horses onward, following in the wake of the head and shoulders preceding us.   But when the head only of the
man appeared above water, our courage failed,
and with one consent we turned back.   We
now clearly saw that this was a ruse of the
wily fellows to decoy the unsuspicious Franks
into the river, where we would inevitably meet
with a watery grave—they themselves in the
mean time reaping their reward on shore, by
possessing themselves of infidel goods and
chattels !

Poor Achmet !   He was sadly lamed by his

struggle in the mad waters, and could not for some time travel as briskly as before, although encouraged by many a kind and sympathizing word from his doting master and rider, the brave Yuseph.

Fortunately, by following the stream a long distance, we at last effected a passage. But it was no easy matter to dismiss the Bedawin, whose provocation at the ill success of their stratagem, vented itself in the most fearful threats and curses.

Suddenly we enter upon one of the loveliest plains on earth—a perfect garden spot—none other than the valley of Sharon. As we ride over its carpet of flowers of every hue and shape, we cannot but obey the irresistible impulse to dismount and pluck them for the leaves of our herbariums. But how sad the reflection that their existence is so ephemeral! There is far more truth than might be supposed in the reputed evanescence of a cer-

5

tain Syrian flower, "that buds, and blooms, and dies within an hour."

We are now approaching Jaffa, the ancient Joppa, supposed to have been founded by Japhet, son of Noah, a small sea-port town of no interest in itself, but fraught with biblical and historical associations of the most stirring nature. It was here that Peter raised to life the charitable Dorcas, and restored her to her astonished friends gathered around her lifeless form. This time-honored place is conspicuously situated on a hill partially defended by a wall, while two-thirds of the base of the hill are washed by the sea.

In the absence of hotels, rooms are taken in the Armenian convent, and, from our windows, we look out upon the sea, and the beautiful orange and lemon groves for which the neighborhood of the town is noted—a quantity of whose golden fruit was lately shipped for Queen Victoria. Our first walk is directed to the house of Simon the tanner, which tradition persists in designating, notwithstanding the frequent overthrows of the town. It agrees in many respects with the Bible narrative. The house of Tabitha is also shown, but, instead of an " upper chamber," we are conducted into a *low cave*. On the south of the town is a spot recalling one of the dark pages of history—the scene of the massacre of the four thousand prisoners, who, upon promise of quarter, surrendered themselves to the mercy of Napoleon, as we are informed by an old resident, from whom we heard the sad tale.

While at Jaffa I had the honor of sitting in the very recess of the wall in which the divan of the Emperor was laid; and, at night, I slept in a window casement overhanging the sea. Such a position may serve very forcibly to remind one of the incident of the young man falling from the window while the Apostle Paul was preaching till midnight and talking till daybreak; but Eutychus could scarcely have tumbled out of such a window as this. Oriental

houses are frequently built with these projecting windows, in which cushions are laid, sometimes serving the double purpose of divan
during the day and bed at night.

Leaving this diluvian city about mid-day, a
few hours' ride brings us to Ramleh, and we are
told by the *reverend fathers,* who extend to us
the hospitality of their convent, that we occupy
the site of the house of Joseph, the rich Arima-
thean.

As we sometimes alight to rest beneath these
great rocks, which become more and more frequent as we approach Jerusalem, we cannot
but recall the expression in the Bible representing the weary traveller seeking the "shadow
of a great rock" as his only refuge from the
scorching rays of a noonday sun. In a thickly
wooded country the shadow of a tree would
very naturally be sought, and in this land,
which abounds in rocks, but is poorly supplied
with trees, the traveller is constantly reminded
of the allusion of the sweet singer of Israel

who penned those beautiful Psalms among these very scenes.

A short distance from Ramleh we pass the site of the city called Lydda in the New Testament, and Ludd by the Arabs, where Eneas was cured by the Apostle Peter. Our path again lay over a rough and mountainous region of country, but we will soon meet with a rich reward for all the toils and fatigue we have been called upon to endure. We are approaching Jerusalem! An hour more and our longing eyes will be greeted with the sight of the holy city; a little while, and our feet shall stand within the gates of "Jerusalem, our happy home!"

A sudden view of swelling domes and towering minarets rising dimly in the distance, causes us to check our horses, and raise our hearts and voices in gratitude to God, while we gaze upon her as "she sits aloft, begirt with battlements." Some of the devout pilgrims of our party fall down in the dust, silently breath-

5 *

ing forth the fullness of their joy; and all seem
to realize the absorbing interest of the moment;
for 'tis an era in our lives never to be forgotten.
On a nearer approach we are enabled to distinguish many of its interesting localities.　The
bold outline of Mount Olivet, crowned with
the Church of Ascension, rising high above
Mount Moriah, on which faithful Abraham
bound his son Isaac to be offered up as a sacri-
fice, occupied subsequently by Solomon's Temple; and Mount Zion, on which the city of
David was built.

> " And throned on her hill sits Jerusalem yet,
>　　But with dust on her forehead and chains on her feet;
> ·For the crown of her pride to the mocker hath gone,
>　　And the holy Shechinah is dark where it shone."

Entering the lofty portal of the Jaffa Gate
(despite the opposition of the rude soldiers,
who seize our horses' bridles, and loudly demand " bucksheesh"), and turning to the left,
we alight at the Latin convent, and are cor-

dially received and ushered into neat and comfortable cells by the monks.

Drenched with the rain, which had fallen nearly all day, and shivering with cold, we called for a fire; and a large chafing dish of charcoal being brought, we closed the door and laid aside our wet garments. But scarcely had we offered thanks for the many and signal deliverances we had experienced from impending danger, when one of our party, dear as life to all of us, suddenly swooned away! As it was immediately suggested that it might be owing to the accumulated carbonic acid of the fire, the door was opened, the gas escaped, and my beloved mother was restored to consciousness. But travellers should be on their guard against charcoal fires in close rooms—several persons having met an untimely death in this same convent, from the inhalation of this noxious gas.

"Nature's sweet restorer, balmy sleep,"

having infused sufficient strength and energy

into our party, we are ready for an excursion, and feel an intense longing to look upon those scenes towards which my imagination in early childhood had gone out like the dove from the hand of Noah, and returned finding no resting-place; but now Mount Zion is before me, Mount Olivet receives the first beams of the rising sun, and I am standing within the walls of the "City of the Great King!"

CHAPTER III.

JERUSALEM.

Let such approach this consecrated land,
    And pass in peace along the magic waste;
But spare its relics—let no busy hand
    Deface the scenes—already how defaced!

BIBLE in hand, we commence the delightful occupation of visiting the interesting localities in and around Jerusalem, held in such deep veneration by Christian, Jew, and Moslem. How fully do we now realize the truths of the Holy Book; and how much greater the pleasure afforded by its sacred pages than heretofore! Here it should be our chief guide-book and constant companion in all our walks; and with the aid of Josephus we may dispense with the services of a voluble Arab guide, whose loud vociferations serve only to distract the

mind and disturb those emotions which are
most enjoyed when alone. When we visit
Bethlehem we shall open at the narrative of
the birth of Christ; at Bethany we will endeavor to sit down with Mary at the feet of
Him who is meek and lowly, and there read
the account of the resurrection of Lazarus; at
Gethsemane the thrilling description of Christ's
agony will stir the deepest feelings of our in-
most souls; and when standing on Calvary and
Olivet, we will turn to the story of his death,
resurrection, ascension, and second coming.

Jerusalem is surrounded with well-preserved
turreted walls, which at intervals are supplied
with square towers. It is situated on four
hills—Zion, Akra, Bezetha, and Moriah; and
is entered by four very imposing gates with
battlements and ramparts, indifferently ornamented with curious devices, among which the
lion is the most conspicuous—emblematic either
of Richard Cœur de Lion, or the Lion of the
tribe of Judah. That known as Bab-es-Sham

ECCE HOMO ARCH

or Damascus Gate, is situated about midway the northern wall. St. Stephen's Gate faces Mount Olivet, and takes its name from its vicinity to the spot upon which that holy martyr is said to have been stoned. No professional pilgrim passes this gate without checking his pace: and lifting up his eyes to the Church of Ascension, he utters a prayer with numerous crossings; nor must he leave the place before he succeeds in finding a flesh-colored limestone, penetrated by veins of reddish hue; for these, they say, were once common limestone, but no sooner had the proto-martyr been stoned to death than they assumed this veiny form in sympathy. Not far distant stands the Golden Gate of the Temple wall, now closed. The Mohammedans have blocked it up in the belief that at some future day, should they neglect this precaution, it would be entered by a king, who would not only take possession of the city but extend his reign over the whole earth. Next is the

Zion Gate on the south, near which, both within and without, the lepers live in their mud huts. Continuing the circuit of the wall we reach the Jaffa Gate on the west, near to which is the custom-house, a coffee-house, and a gambling establishment, the principal "gathering-place" of the city.

Besides these four gates, which are always kept open from sunrise to sunset, except an hour at mid-day on Friday, the Mohammedan Sabbath, there are several others; but they are all now walled up, except the Mugrabin Gate in the Cheesmongers' Valley, which is kept open whenever there is a scarcity of water in the city, in order to shorten the communication with the Virgin's Fount, the Pool of Siloam, and the Well of Nehemiah Yuab, or En-rogel. The present "el-Khuds," or the Holy, would appear to occupy only about one-third of the city under its largest dimensions, at the date of its destruction. The whole of Mount Ophel, and about one-half of Mount

Zion, are excluded on the south, and nearly all of Cœnopolis on the north. But its breadth, so far as it extends, is about the same that it was in its *palmiest* days.

Entering the city at the Jaffa Gate, and taking a southerly direction, we will glance at the principal objects of interest as we pass along.

On the right is a group of square towers, called in the language of tradition the Fortress of David—one of which is undoubtedly the frowning Tower of Hippicus. In strong contrast with these massive old towers, is the light gothic church just opposite, in which the English and Prussian missionaries worship. Just in the rear of this church are the ruins of the Church of Yacobeiah (James the Less), which is well worth a visit as a relic of the crusaders' days. A little further on is the Church of St. James, in connection with an immense convent, both belonging to the Armenians. This church is said to mark the spot

6

where the Apostle James was beheaded by
Herod. It is gaudily adorned with pictures
and figures of numberless saints, profusely be-
decked with jewels; and the ceiling is hung
with festoons of ostrich eggs. But its chief
ornament is a door entirely encased with
mother-of-pearl and tortoise shell. Passing
through an archway beneath the palace of the
Armenian Patriarch, and continuing along this
street, we have on our left the hospital and
printing establishment of the Armenians, and
soon reach the Zion Gate, outside of which is
another Armenian church, said to contain the
true door of the Holy Sepulchre—the stone
with which the tomb of Joseph of Arimathea
was closed. Near by us is the Cœnaculum, in
that curious aggregation of buildings called
Neby Daûd, or Tomb of David, covering the
spot on which tradition says the Lord's supper
was instituted. Here, also, in this huge pile,
tradition locates the villa of Caiaphas. All this
part of the hill is covered with the burying

ground of the Greeks, Armenians, and Latins, and a small enclosure containing the tombs of several American missionaries and travellers lies in the shadow of the Tomb of David. Its location is greatly objected to by the Turks, who are greatly scandalized by its propinquity to the remains of their great prophet David, and are very loth to allow the interment of *infidel Christian dogs,* near their holy mosque. It is the property of the American Board of Commissioners for Foreign Missions.

As we pass through the gate our hearts are sickened at the sight of the loathsome lepers, who stretch forth their fingerless hands, or handless arms, for charity. Such ravages has the disease made upon these poor creatures, that some of them are without noses, and almost without mouths—the mere wreck of human beings—so hideous that we toss them a coin from as great a distance as possible! But however importunate in their plaintive cries for bucksheesh, they never come near you,

but stand "afar off" in most entreating attitude, as of old, when "Jesus entered into a
certain village there met him ten men that
were lepers, which stood afar off, and lifted up
their voices and said, Jesus, Master, have
mercy on us."

Continuing in the same direction without the
city walls, a narrow path brings us to the lofty
angle of the wall surrounding the Temple enclosure, and then winds along the edge of a
Mohammedan cemetery, distinguished from
those of the Jews and Christians by a repre-
sentation in stone of a turban at the head of
each tomb.

Re-entering the city by St. Stephen's Gate,
we tread the narrow mazes of the Via Dolorosa
or Doleful Way, along which the Saviour is said
to have carried the cross as he went out to be
crucified. A little way within the gate is a deep
trench, thought by some to be the Pool of Bethesda, and just opposite is the Church of St.
Anne, in which it is said the Virgin Mary

was born; and a few steps farther on the left is the residence of the Governor of Jerusalem, once the abode of Pilate, but not at all palatial in its present dilapidated condition.

This place is now called " Serai" or the Seraglio, and is unquestionably the site of the Fortress of Antonia. All travellers who choose to take advantage of the privilege, are admitted into the Governor's presence, and after the usual round of salaams, coffee, pipes, and bucksheeshes, they are conducted to the roof of the house, which overlooks the sunny grounds of the Temple enclosure.

In walking through the city one is struck with the peculiar structure of the doors of the courts of the convents, and some other buildings, consisting of a very small door cut through a large one: the smaller being kept open at all times, and the larger occasionally, for the ingress and egress of horses and camels, and not unfrequently a caravan. This may illustrate the figure used by Christ in three of the

6 *

Gospels : " It is easier for a camel to go through the eye of a needle than for a rich man to enter the kingdom of God :" the large door being the needle, and the small opening, through which a camel could not possibly enter, its eye.

Over many of the doors are sculptures and paintings, accompanied with inscriptions in Arabic. These attest that the owner has made a pilgrimage to Mecca, and hence is entitled to the honorable appellation of " Hadji," a designation of which its possessor is always very proud.

This street abounds in " holy places"—here a blocked-up doorway to the " Sancta Scala," leading into Antonia; a little further on an indentation in the stone wall is seriously alleged to have been made by the cross of Christ when resting against it; hard by is the house of Veronica, whence started the Wandering Jew on his never ending pilgrimage; and there, a high overspanning arch upon which our Lord is con-

fidently affirmed to have stood when Pilate
showed him to the people, and cried " Ecce
homo !" "Behold the man !"

But, before passing beneath the arch, we
pass on the right the " Church of Flagellation."
Numberless almost are the localities with which
the Romish monks have connected some incident of the New Testament record; over
nearly all of which is erected a church, a convent, or at least a little chapel, decorated with
hideous pictures and gaudy tinsel.

A few yards below the Ecce Homo Arch, on
the left, is an old ruined church; and at the
corner, where the Via Dolorosa turns to the
left, is a fine building, in a tolerable state of
preservation, called, and for aught I know, correctly, King Baldwin's Bath. Wonderingly,
we notice that everybody wearing a Christian
garb, kisses a rough stone bowl, conspicuously
standing by itself, hard by a house rather
larger and better than the surrounding dwellings. The bowl, we are gravely told, is that

used by Lazarus, though it is so heavy that a dozen men could scarcely carry it; and the house, though evidently of modern construction, the dwelling of Dives.

In one of these houses a curious incident lately occurred. During the visit of a Frank lady to Jerusalem, she was awakened one night by loud screams and heartrending cries of distress from female voices in the house just opposite her lodgings. She could in no way account for them, except under the impression that some tyrannical barbarian of a Turk was exercising his cruelty upon some half dozen of his wives. A Frank battery of stones was immediately opened upon the Moslem castle, and all noise ceasing within after less than five minutes cannonading, our heroine retreated; and the remainder of the night was spent, mayhap, in the restlessness and disquietude of a troubled spirit. Horrible scenes of bastinading, if not bloodshed, had been called up by every piercing cry; and, in the conscientious discharge of her duty, she had firmly resolved to do all in her power to redress the wrongs of her suffering and helpless sisters. The morning, however, brought with it a satisfactory explanation. A member of the family had died, and, as is the universal custom, friends had assembled to evince their grief by tearing their hair, beating their breasts, and unitedly shrieking aloud. It was a mournful scene like this, perhaps, at which Christ was present, when a multitude were gathered in the house of the ruler of the synagogue, to weep over the death of his daughter. "He beheld a tumult, and them that wept and wailed greatly." And when Christ was besought by the ruler to restore his daughter to life, he said: "Why are ye making an outcry and weeping? The damsel is not dead, but sleepeth."

Notwithstanding the devotion paid at the "Shrine of the Bowl" by the Christian, the deportment of the Jew is quite the reverse— for in passing he contemptuously spits upon it;

but both are laughed at by the self-conceited Mohammedan, who despises the religion of each.

Among all the so-called "sacred localities," the Church of the Holy Sepulchre is considered as first in importance. This spot has been marked by some kind of monument ever since A. D. 326, when the Empress Helena made a pilgrimage to the Holy City at the advanced age of threescore years and ten, and erected a number of church edifices. Whether it has been correctly located or not, has been a matter of much dispute. Thousands of pilgrims, however, give full testimony to the sincerity of their faith by surmounting every difficulty, and travelling great distances, for the sake of worshipping at the holy shrine. The faith of the most devout and credulous pilgrim must, however, be put to the severest test, when he finds the reputed site of the crucifixion and resurrection in the very heart of the city, instead of being without the walls, as we learn that it evidently was, both from the Old Testament and the New. But, notwithstanding this inexplicable difficulty, we can but yield ourselves unresistingly to the *impression*, even though it be a delusion, that this is none other than the site of the most soul-affecting tragedy ever recorded in the annals of time or the cycles of eternity. And I envy not the heart of that individual, who can enter the tomb, alleged to have been that of the Son of God, and feel not emotions that he had never felt before, even though he may feel oppressed with doubts of its reality.

Determined not to be outdone by the Christians, and with the special intention of annoying them, the Mohammedans have erected two tall minarets—one in front and the other in the rear of the Church of the Holy Sepulchre—from the tops of which the five citations of the muezzim are daily wafted over the Christian dome.

The remains of various churches are found clustering around this great monumental church edifice, most conspicuous amongst which are those of Maria Minor and Maria Major—the Lesser and Greater Marys. With one exception—that of the shambles on Mount Zion—the most repulsive and noisome spot in all Jerusalem is that sink of filth called a tannery, contiguous to the church buildings on the east, specially designed by the Turks to annoy the Christians. Strong indeed must be the olfactories of the pilgrim who would visit the beautiful remains of the Palace of the Knights of St. John, situated just opposite, though so well repaying a protracted exploration. The Emperor of the French, to whom the Sultan has lately presented these fine remains, and the large lot to which they appertain, will have quite a task in cleansing this Augean stable!

While, in this neighborhood, the enlightened traveller, who would form a just estimate of the value of oral tradition in the ascertainment of the sacred localities, would do well to visit an old olive *tree*, which we are assured, by the blind guides of Jerusalem, is the identical *bush* in which the horns of Isaac's vicarious victim were entangled when Abraham was about to offer up "his son—his only son Isaac whom he loved." Now, although this spot is on Akra, instead of Moriah, where that memorable transaction is recorded to have occurred, yet thousands of credulous pilgrims every year worship at this tree in the full assurance that it is the identical bush alluded to, notwithstanding it grows upon the ground floor of an old ruined house beneath which is a cellar and a tank of water. Somewhere hereabouts they also show to a certain class of pilgrims—those who have the bumps of ignorance, superstition, and legendary faith, well developed—something still more marvellous—the "stone that the builders rejected!" and something stranger still—reader, what do you think it is? The "gallus canticus!" yes, the veritable "cock that crew" when Peter so shamefully fell! I have not seen either of

7

these *sacred relics,* but have no special reason
to doubt that they are thus exhibited to pilgrims whose sanctity is of the right odor.
But Palestine is not the only clime in which
the exuberant plant of superstition thrives; for
surely neither of these is half so monstrous as
the "*sancta scala,*" or "sacred ladder," trans-
ferred to Rome, *down which the Saviour was
conducted from judgment,* on whose large stone
steps I saw many poor pilgrims crawling bare-
kneed! or the House of "our Lady" borne to
Loretto on angels' wings! How can oral tradi-
tionists, who believe in these silly Munchausen
legends, find it in their hearts, or their sleeves,
to laugh at the Moslems for believing that the
large rock in the Temple yard commenced its
flight toward Heaven on the occasion of Mohammed's celebrated Hegira, and was only pre-
vented accompanying the prophet by the strong
hands of angels holding it in its place!

Leaving the vicinity of the Church of the
Holy Sepulchre, and descending Palmer Street

a few yards farther, we enter the main thoroughfare of the city, leading from the Damascus Gate to that of Zion—upon which are situated the principal bazaars. What motley throngs of human beings!—if, indeed, all those bipeds passing before us may be honored with such a designation. What a ferocious-looking animal is that scowling Bedawin sheikh! but proud and scornful as he is, he is compelled to give way before the haughty Turk and do him homage. But what poor half-naked women are those sitting along the bazaars selling charcoal, parsley, snails, eggs, and fruits, and vegetables of every kind,—shamelessly unveiled? They are the fellahin women—the serfs of Palestine and Syria. Upon these poor creatures devolves nearly all the drudgery of farming and trafficking. To see one of these tawny females trudging to market, bearing a large basket of fruit, vegetables, or poultry, while she swings her infant in a sack on her back, and carries her next

youngest astride her shoulder, and her liege
lord riding before her, leisurely smoking his
pipe, is not an uncommon sight. Nor does it
excite the slightest degree of surprise or pity.
What a clattering the clogs make upon the
pavement—if such we may call the smooth
rocks of every size and shape that lie here and
there in the street; but they are an admirable
contrivance for the ankle-deep mud of Jerusalem streets, and one very generally worn by
the lower classes during the winter. It may
be well to turn aside just here to examine the
operations practised by silversmiths, braziers,
and other metal mongers. How odd that pack-
mule appears—with a woman and child in a
basket on one side counterpoising several large
children on the other! Clear the track for
that long string of camels laden with brush-
wood from Hebron! "Dahrac! Dahrac!" cries
the camel driver, "your back! your back!"
and gladly do you retreat into any alley or
recess near at hand. But did ever anybody

see so many cats out of Kilkenny! and such
droves of dogs. These, like the bipedal inhabitants, have peculiar districts which they
rigidly guard; and woe betide the poor canine
that incautiously crosses the line! And when
a regular pitched battle is fought with two
or three scores of belligerents on either side,
an awful yelling and howling is the consequence. This toleration of dogs and cats on
the part of Mussulmans is not a little strange,
inasmuch as the contact of a dog renders them
unclean, and imposes on them the necessity
of purification by ablution. But who is this
strange degraded-looking wretch who is receiving such demonstrations of respect and reverence from all classes of the Mohammedans, not
excepting the highest effendis and dignitaries
both of church and state—kissing his hands
and invoking his blessing? He is naked, with
the exception of a single piece of a garment;
but seems to be a welcome visiter everywhere.
Happy fellow! he is a "mejnoon," either an

7 *

idiot or a harmless lunatic; and all such are held in high esteem!

We are now in the pipe-making bazaar, where so many hands are constantly employed; for every one smokes in Jerusalem, from the old Pasha down to the youngest girl! It is due, however, both to Turk, Jew, and Christian, to record it to their praise that there is not a single tobacco chewer in all the Holy City and Holy Land, except a few European or American Jews and Christians! But what sort of a character is that, with a well filled goatskin on his back, and various vessels appended on both sides—clashing his brazen pans together as he threads the crowd—lauding the excellence of his beverages! He is a walking fountain: and pours forth water both sweet and bitter! drinks of all sorts: sherbet, lemonade, and sweetened scented water, and even arrak for the *Christian!* But great as the crowd is, it must now scamper, and give way to what seems to be divers stacks of weeds, briars, and

brush, which move mysteriously up the street;
but upon close inspection, you perceive buried
underneath the huge mass a small donkey by
which it is borne—reminding you of the
world upon the shoulders of Atlas. Such is
the fuel of the Jerusalem bakeries, though
the kitchens are supplied with charcoal brought
from Hebron. But here comes another character, with whom we are almost as careful to
avoid a collision as with the briars and brambles.
He is a professional oil man, retailing oil from
his goatskin bottle, and every rag about him is
perfectly saturated with oil; and it almost
seems to ooze from his body. Here we meet
one of the Jerusalem celebrities. He has come,
like the Jew, to die at the Holy City. But he
is a Christian; has visions and revelations;
believes himself the Elijah that was to come;
has flags ready to deliver to the restored Jews,
as soon as they reach Jaffa; has doffed the
Frank dress, and assumed the oriental costume
-—taking Abraham as his model in manners,

customs, &c. Poor fellow! his change of dress had well nigh cost him his life: he was passing the court of the Holy Sepulchre on a certain occasion, and concluded to go in; but no sooner had he entered the court than he was pursued by the Christians, and only saved his life by seizing the cross that hung from the girdle of a priest, who was beating him to death, and devoutly kissing it—thus conclusively proving that he was not a Jew. There are many such characters in the Holy City—and exceedingly religious they are—but they certainly have a very curious way of showing it.

Having wandered through the city, and weary of the confined air and crowded streets, we long for the green fields and the pleasant walks to be enjoyed outside the walls; for until we have seen Gethsemane, ascended Mount Olivet, and visited Bethany, we shall feel restless and impatient, and unable to realize fully that we are in the land of the Saviour and his Apostles.

CHAPTER IV.

WALK AROUND THE WALLS.

"I tread where the Twelve in their wayfaring trod;
  I stand where they stood with the chosen of God—
  Where his blessings were heard and his lessons were taught,
  And the blind were restored and the healing was wrought."

GLAD, again to escape the narrow lanes and confined air of the city, we make our exit through the Jaffa Gate, with difficulty edging our way through a noisy crowd of soldiers and Fellahin, and it may be, a caravan, trying to effect an entrance into the city, this gate being more constantly used than any of the others. The soldiers who guard it are looked upon with no little dread by the country people, upon whom they lay a heavy tax for every basket of vegetables, fruit, and fowls, brought into the city. Outside, a lively scene usually presents itself. To the right are the café and custom-house, patronized by crowds of Jews, Turks, and Christians, engaged in smoking and gaming. To the left, is the justly dreaded quarantine station, which is nothing more nor less than the deep fosse of the fortifications of the city castle; but, inappropriate as it may seem, it is yet far more seemly than its late location, which was in the famous Grotto of Jeremiah, near the Damascus Gate, beneath a Turkish cemetery! Even yon Egyptian pilgrim, who has just escaped its "durance vile," must have suffered dreadfully from the hot sun in such an oven.

Following the road to the Convent of the Cross for a quarter of a mile, we reach the so called Upper Pool of Gihon, affording a favorite bathing-place for the residents of the city. Around it are many lookers-on, vastly amused with the aquatic feats of the bathers. Near it are the vaults of the "Charnel House of the Lion," filled with human skulls, thrown in, pell-mell, it is said, by Ibrahim Pacha. On some

EN ROGEL AND VALLEY OF JEHOSAPHAT.

of them tufts of hair are left, for the purpose of
drawing them up into heaven. A little way
from the path is a wely or small white building erected over the grave of a celebrated saint.
These are everywhere to be seen in the East,
and bring to mind the whited sepulchres, to
which the Saviour compared the hypocrisy of
the Scribes and Pharisees. It has been face-
tiously remarked, by a celebrated traveller in
Palestine, that wherever he went he saw these
monuments to dead Moslem saints—" but
where," says he, " are the living ones?"

A funeral procession may now be seen passing, in the centre of which is a corpse, carried
on a litter by four men. The form of the
coffin is made to resemble, as nearly as possible, that of a human being. It is covered with
drapery, and surmounted with the green turban
of the Osmanlis. Arab women with naked
busts, hair dishevelled and flowing over their
shoulders, and their faces and breasts bruised,
precede the corpse. With arms thrown up into

the air, they shriek and sing their doleful
death-songs.   These mourning women are
alluded to by Jeremiah, when he says :—

> " Give ear, call the mourning women that they come,
>   And to the skilful, send that they come ;
>   Let them hasten and lift up the lamentation over us."

Next is a company of musicians, playing a
funeral dirge on the tom-tom.   In front are
the veiled women, near relatives of the deceased, who, after the burial, make daily visits
to the grave, to utter their piercing death-
songs, and deposit a plate of sweetmeats on
the grave-stone, as a means of reconciling angels
to the wicked deeds committed during the lifetime of the deceased.   No remains of the food
being found next day, they believe it has
afforded a dainty morsel for offended angels,
whereas it has been appropriated by famished
jackals or starving beggars.   They carry this
extravagant funeral pomp to a still greater

extent, by tearing out their hair, and throwing dust on their heads.

Following this valley downward we observe, on the hill overhanging the lower " Pool of Gihon," the veritable tree on which Judas is said to have hung himself! It stands on the ruins of the house of Caiaphas, and its size strikes one as rather diminutive, after a growth of eighteen centuries; we therefore look upon it with rather an incredulous eye, albeit so admirably adapted to the purpose by its gibbet-like shape. Immediately above, overhanging the deep gorge of the lower portion of the Hinnom valley, is the field of Aceldama, whose earth *is said* to consume the flesh of the bodies committed to it in forty-eight hours! A portion of this hill is called the " Hill of Evil Council," where Judas and the betrayers of our Lord consulted as to the manner in which they might take him. Many tombs are excavated in the sides of the hill, some of very fine workmanship, with painted ceilings and ornamental

8

carvings. In one the furniture of a devout pilgrim was found, who had gone there to do penance and die. Near his skeleton (?) was a can, supposed to have contained water, another for oil perhaps, and other articles of this description, besides numerous relics and pictures of saints.

Squads of Turkish women may be seen among the olive trees enjoying a "phantazeia," or pic-nic; and the valley resounds with their sharp quavering notes of joy, which are very peculiar. They suddenly raise their voices from the lowest monotone to the highest imaginable pitch, and interrupt the sounds by repeatedly throwing their hands against their mouths.

At the end of the valley of the Tyropœon is the Pool of Siloam, with its five venerated columns. These are thought by some to identify this pool with the Bethesda of old, where the "blind, halt, withered, and other impotent folk" were healed of whatsoever disease they had, rather than that within the city. A little higher up (in the valley of the "dark Kedron") is the "Virgin's Fount"—a dark underground pool, into which women are constantly descending to fill their jugs and skin-bottles with its cool transparent water, while some are engaged in washing their clothes by the singular process of pounding them with rounded stones. A few paces below are the "Kings' Gardens," even now fit pleasure grounds for royalty, with rich green foliage, and crimson and yellow fruit of pomegranate and orange groves. Near by (at the mouth of the Cheesemongers' Valley), standing on a heap of stones and rubbish, is the tree on which Isaiah is said to have been sawn asunder!—a venerable, decrepid old mulberry tree, under whose refreshing shade lazy Arabs spend a large portion of the year—day and night.

Situated a short distance below, at the confluence of the valleys of Hinnom and Kedron, is the Well of Joab, affording an abundant sup-

ply of living water during the whole year. At
the annual overflowing of the well, the inhabitants of the city repair hither to have a pic-
nic on the green banks of the rushing stream.
They bring their culinary utensils, and either
pitch tents or place rugs where they lazily loll
and smoke their pipes.

Changing our course we proceed northward,
up the Valley of Jehosaphat, the former bed of
the brook where

> " Kedron's slender rill,
> That bathed His feet, as to His lowly work
> Of mercy He went forth, still kept His name
> Securely hoarded in its secret fount,
> A precious pearl-drop !"

On the western slope of the Hill of Scandal
is the sepulchral village of Silwan. Here excavations that were originally intended for the
dead, are now appropriated by the living for
their dwelling-places. The manner of burying
the dead, to which reference is made throughout the Bible, corresponds exactly with the

sepulchres which are found in the East at the present day. In these accounts we are told they were "hewn out of a rock." Sarah was buried in the cave of Machpelah. These sepulchres exist everywhere; the rocky sides of the hills are full of such excavations, some of which are so extensive, and chiselled with such care, they are now converted into dwelling-places of the living, as is the case with this village, whose inhabitants live quite contentedly in the dark, damp tombs of which it is almost entirely composed.

We pause, and gaze with wonder at the immense stones in the angle of the Temple wall, towering above. Jutting from this part of the wall, at an elevation of sixty or seventy feet, is the traditional seat of Mohammed, to be occupied by him on the final day of reckoning, when he is to judge the assembled universe in the "Valley of Decision" below. Every Moslem, in virtue of his true faith, will walk over this valley on a slender iron wire, which leads him

8 *

on the other side the gulf into Paradise. But the "infidel" Jews and Christians are mercilessly consigned to the world of punishment by the fiat of his omnipotent will.

The valley is here spanned by a small bridge; and in the base of Olivet, on the other side of the valley, are the legendary tombs of Zechariah, Jehosaphat, and St. James, and the pillar of Absalom. They are hewn out of the solid rock, and the latter is surmounted with a tall cupola of fantastic form. The devout pilgrim of every creed always pelts this monument with stones on passing it, accompanied by fearful curses, to show his abhorrence of the sin of filial disobedience of which Absalom affords such a lamentable example. This is the ground allotted to the Jews for the burial of their dead. The tombs are nothing more than unsculptured stones, laid flat on the ground, with an occasional inscription in Hebrew. The highest ambition of every Jew, of whatever clime, is a resting-place in this soil—hallowed by associations so dear to his heart.

A hundred or two yards farther is the Garden of Gethsemane, and close by, the subterranean Church of the Virgin Mary, adorned with lamps, flowers, and pictures, the usual furniture of a Romish chapel. It is dark and damp, and its worshippers go about like so many spectres through its cavernous recesses, at the heels of a priest, waving censer, and making the sign of the cross before each dumb picture and idolatrously revered relic.

Following the meanderings of the valley some distance higher, through many gardens and by many tombs, we decline to the left, and a short distance from the valley, reach the Tombs of the Kings—a succession of sepulchres with an elaborately carved entrance. In the walls, recesses are cut for the reception of sarcophagi, or stone coffins, and, in some of the chambers, there are remains of these coffins themselves, which once no doubt contained the

bodies of royalty. Our exploration is not without its physical discomforts, for the doorways
to these dark inner chambers are so low that
an entrance is only to be effected by the low-
liest of attitudes, and the ground is most uncomfortably damp, if not actually muddy.

The rolling away of the stone, mentioned in
connection with the Saviour's resurrection, is
clearly explained by a discovery lately made at
the entrance of these tombs, where it is seen,
from indications now exposed by late excavations of the ground, that an arrangement of this
kind once existed. This interesting discovery
was lately made by my father, and great was
his delight when, with the help of a pickaxe,
he removed an artificial floor of rubbish, and
beheld the exact counterpart of the door of
Christ's sepulchre. A small doorway is cut in
the wall, and, by an ingenious arrangement, a
thick stone disk fits over the door, and can be
rolled away at pleasure. And it is thus that
many passages of Scripture are explained by

late exhumations in connection with the manners and customs of the present inhabitants of Syria. The most careless tourist cannot fail to be constantly reminded that he is travelling in the land of the Bible. As for the infidel, 'twere strange indeed were he to retain aught of skepticism after visiting this land that contains so many convincing proofs of the truth of Revelation.

Having almost completed the circuit of the city, and passed over the most interesting ground immediately around the walls, we pursue the stony path leading to the Damascus Gate. Before entering the city, however, we visit the Cave of Jeremiah, lying immediately in our way. This is a grotto in which the lugubrious prophet is said to have lived, and to which he retreated after the deportation of the Jews by the Assyrians. On the side of the steep street, leading from this gate, we encounter a crowd of idlers surrounding a blind storyteller seated on a rude divan of stones. Here he may be found at all hours of the day, and the delighted countenances of his listeners show how much they are amused with his wonderful stories.

The gates of city walls were very important structures before the invention of gunpowder, when battering-rams and balista supplied the place of cannon, and were generally constructed after the manner of towers. Of such structures we have an instance in the remains of this gate. There is every reason to believe it is the gate mentioned by Nehemiah as an " old gate" even in his day ; and hence must be regarded as one of the oldest pieces of architecture about the Holy City—exceeded in antiquity only by the remains of Solomon's Bridge and the Temple wall. The cut opposite represents the tower room adjoining the gate on the east, which is in a better state of preservation than that on the west. The upper portions of this room are of comparatively modern construction—the work probably either of the Saracens,

Turks, or Crusaders; but the lower courses of stones, which are quite colossal, undoubtedly occupy the position in which they were placed by the Jews, in the palmy days of the Holy City, and afford an excellent specimen of Jewish mural architecture. It contains, in the wall of its western side, a hollow spiral stairway, which is the only one ever discovered; and, as it serves to explain the " winding stairway" of the Temple, which has never heretofore been understood, it may be well to describe it. It is constructed entirely in the substance of the western wall of the room, which is very thick. It is built around a square pillar, about two feet in thickness, and contains room enough for two or three persons to pass at a time. In the foreground, near the two Greek Christians, is seen a stone slab which probably served as a trap door above. The low entrance to the stairway is seen on the left—being merely a vacancy made by leaving out two rocks in the two lower courses of masonry—the door to which was probably an immense rock of that exact size, with which it could be easily blocked up on occasion—in time of siege. This stairway being constructed entirely in the thickness of the wall, the "watchman on the walls of Zion" could at any time descend into this room unobserved.

How many palpitating hearts have quailed and failed in this very room! History records more than thirty sieges that Jerusalem has undergone, and often has it been captured, and not unfrequently its mighty walls in part overthrown.

How many famous kings and warriors have passed the portals of this same "Old Gate!" How many wise men and magistrates have sat within it giving counsel and ministering justice; and how many myriads of reverent youth have here bowed the head to hoary age, as they passed in and out! But now the only dignitary that passes it is the haughty Pacha: it is guarded by the surly Turk, who neither gives nor receives counsel or justice; and the venerable elders of Israel, instead of homage, receive only insult and injury at the hands of the youth, either of Turks, Arabs, or Christians!

This gate is at present called by the natives Bab-el-Amûd, Gate of the Pillar, and Bab-es-Sham, or Syria, of which Damascus is the capital. Occupying, as it does, the lowest part of the valley crossed by the wall where it was so easily attacked, it was doubtless made one of the strongest fortifications about Jerusalem. It was no doubt in view of such cyclopean structures as this, that the seer of Anathoth so plaintively bemoaned the fate of the fallen city, saying: "The kings of the earth, all the inhabitants of the world, would not have believed that the adversary and the enemy should have entered into the gates of Jerusalem."

No one, in walking around the city walls, fails to notice the picturesque portion just opposite Jeremiah's Cave, and near Damascus

9

Gate. Built upon a bold and prominent rock, and towering high above other portions of the walls, it is conspicuous from every point. Just here is the entrance to a remarkable cave, which has created much wonder and surmise. On scrambling through the small hole leading to the cave, my father and brothers (who were the fortunate discoverers of the cave) found themselves in a vast hall, with a vaulted roof, supported by numbers of natural pillars. Their visit was made under the protecting mantle of night, in order to evade the eye of the jealous Turk. Leaving the city about nightfall, they secreted themselves near the walls, and waited until long after they heard the closing of the great iron-covered leaves of the Damascus Gate, before venturing on the exploration.

In their wanderings through the dark cavern, the light of their torches fell upon a human skeleton. It lay in the bottom of a deep and precipitous pit, making more awful the stillness of the night, and adding tenfold to the fearfulness of the scene. This was, perhaps, the skeleton of an explorer, insufficiently supplied with light; and coming unconsciously upon the verge of the pit, was, without a moment's warning, precipitated headlong down the frightful chasm. Fortunately for our more provident explorers, they were well supplied with lights, enabling them to make a less sudden transit to its rocky floor, where they possessed themselves of the fractured skull, as an agreeable memento of this very agreeable place!

Along the intricate passages, through the vast white halls, they roamed the greater part of the night—now seating themselves to rest in a sub-grotto, which, anywhere else, and at any other time, would be a most lovely little retreat; and now gazing with wonder at the colossal pillars; themselves and the flitting bats being the sole living intruders upon the solitude of this gloomy place.

Besides the white pile of human bones, there were smaller heaps strewn about, which, upon

examination, proved to be the skeletons of
animals brought in by jackals—the real pro-
prietors of the cave; and here let me give
honor to whom honor is due. Our dog had
first attracted our attention to the cavern by
scenting a jackal at its mouth; and to this
noblest of the canine race must really be
awarded the palm of discovery.

This, it is thought, is the quarry from which
the stone was hewn for the erection of the
Temple.

Heavy masses of rock hanging from the
ceiling accounted for a shock which we had
felt, while living just at the extremity of the
cave, which we mistook at the time for an
earthquake. One of these rocks had no doubt
fallen, causing the whole hill to shake and
tremble, as well as its affrighted inhabitants.

This mammoth cavern has not only troubled
the mind of the antiquary with theory and
speculation, but has inspired the poet, and
called forth the graphic lines here given from

the pen of the gifted author* of the "Cave of Machpelah," and other poems:—

ADDRESS TO THE TEMPLE-QUARRY OF SOLOMON.

I.

Thou ancient quarry, hidden from the sun
Since the proud day of princely Solomon!
Within thy awful depths there long had lain
In embryo,—the temple's sacred fane;—
Like the bright forms, the eye of genius sees
Robed in the marble of Praxiteles.

II.

I stand and look upon your dusty bed
In silent awe, with reverential head,
And see the marks, as of the recent line
In tracery clear, in all their freshness shine;
As if the hand that drew them still was nigh,
And suddenly had vanished from our eye—
Here fragments, pile on pile, promiscuous shown
The clippings bright from off the flinty stone.
And as I gaze, I wonder why they stay,
Nor hasten to the labors of the day;
And people in my thoughts the busy throng
Delving the labyrinthine crypts among.
Perhaps through gloomy caverns now they creep,
Or some high festival they joyous keep;

* James Challen.

9 *

Or, while some distant king has come to view
Their vast designs ; they give him homage due.

III.

Ere the huge hammer struck your flinty walls,
Or busy workman thronged your ample halls ;
Or a rude block, was chiselled by their hands
To sink the base, on which the temple stands ;—
Here was Araunah's threshing floor ; the place
On which he lowly bowed his reverent face
To David ; when, the direful plague to stay,
The king to build an altar, vowed that day.
" Take it as thine, and let my chosen Lord
Fulfil his sacred purpose and his word ;
Nay," said the king, " it shall not hence be thought
I give to God, that which has cost me nought."
And, like the " Friend of God," he weighed the gold,
And the last mite, the price in full he told.

IV.

Lo ! from thy bed I see a form arise
Sublime and beautiful ; as if the skies
Had sent their master builders to the earth,
And by a word divine, had giv'n it birth !
Or like to him, who in the sepulchre
In after times, felt the deep mighty stir
Of the all-quickening Spirit, on that morn
In which our glorious hope of life was born.

The deep foundations and the massive walls
Now sink; then rise the ample halls,—
Pillar and arch and stately corridor,
Leading to distant chambers—floor on floor,
Until the glorious temple kiss'd the sky.
No sound of hammer heard—but rising silently.

v.

Ages have fled, the Syrian kings have swept
Down to the dust, where the brave warriors slept
Of Israel's tribes; the leopard, hungry for his spoil,
Has fiercely trodden down her sacred soil;
And the wild beasts, with eyes like men, have trod
Prophet and priest beneath the blushing sod.
Persian and Parthian, and the hated race
Of Moab and of Edom, fighting face to face;
And the fierce Maccabees, with brother's blood
Have soaked its valleys with a crimson flood.
Roman, and Turk, and Christian, all have striven
To blot thy name, O, Zion, under heaven!
But vain their efforts, still a power unknown
Watches thy dust, where once the temple shone.
And here within this secret quarry lies
A symbol of thy fallen greatness; and our eyes
Look on this giant frame, with hope and trust
And hear it speaking thus, from out the dust:—

    " Long centuries have passed away,
      Since in this crypt I slumbering lay;

Their onward tread I anxious heard ;
And oft in fear and doubt was stirred
When battling hosts and clashing arms
Spread ruin wide and mad alarms.
But never did my beating heart
Throb with such anguish, or did start
As at that fierce and maddening cry,
 Of ' Crucify ! Crucify !'
When God's own Son was doomed to die.
My dusty limbs, like a wreck at sea,
Shook as if tossed on a shelving lee,
  When I heard
   The word
  ' My God ! O why
Hast thou forsaken me !' "

VI.

"The walls of my prison were rent and torn,
And the mountain masses were upwards borne ;
And I deemed that the earth by tempests riven
Was wrecked by the threaten'd wrath of heaven.
The silence that followed was deep as the grave,
As the gathering darkness, wave on wave
Fell on the Temple, the city, the land,
And terror was spreading on every hand.
Then a fierce seething stroke from the o'erburdened cloud
Rent the vail of the Temple, at that " cry" long and loud !
The shades in the under-world startled with fear,
And deemed that the judgment-sign soon would appear ;

And the saints who for ages in dust found repose,
Awoke and came forth when the conq'ror arose,
And appeared in the city to many—then fled
To their silent retreats, 'mong the time-honored dead.
And here as I lay in my rock-girded prison,
I heard voices say, "Christ is risen—is risen!"
Gentle footsteps of women, then passing along
Through the old dusky streets and the by-paths among;
They talk'd low and sadly, and feared to delay,
As they said, "Who for us will the stone roll away?
With these spices we've bought to our Master we go,
For the dead, not the living, these symbols we show."

VII.

Clear and cold was the night; on the murmuring streams
The morning star shed all the wealth of its gleams,
And the dew falling thick on the brow and the crest
Of the mail-covered soldier, now taking his rest.
Profound was the silence; on the city it fell
Like the low-breathing pulses of ocean's vast swell,
Rising gently, then falling, as if the old deep
Of its heavings was weary, and sinking to sleep.
When lo! a keen light pierced the clefts in these walls,
Startling quickly the owl and the bat from its halls;
And I knew it had come not from sun or from star,
But it came from a region still lovelier far.
As an earthquake, that shakes the deep mountain's stronghold,
So I heard when the stone from the tomb was then rolled,

When the Saviour, who died to relieve all our woes,
Conquered death and the grave, and in triumph arose.
How I strove then to shiver the old rusty chains,
A captive long held in my dark prison pains!
Each bone struck its kindred; and my dry-wither'd tongue
" Victory!" fain would have shouted—in raptures have sung.
Quivering joy shook this dust; and my meaningless eyes
In their wide starless sockets were struck with surprise.
But more feeble than infancy—heavy as night,
Death still held me a prey to his marvellous might;
But I thought then I heard, in the loftiest strains,
Angel minstrels now singing those heaven-taught pæans:

    " Christ the Lord has come to save,
       And has risen from the grave;
       Death is conquered, heaven is won,
       See, the glorious work is done.
       To the realms of endless day
       Now he shows to us the way;
       Men and angels join to sing
       Christ th' anointed Lord and King.
       Honor, majesty divine,
       On thy head shall ever shine;
       And thy mitre and thy crown
       Nations yet unborn shall own.
       And the dead, both small and great,
       Who in dust and ashes wait,
       On the land and in the sea,
       By their Ransom shall be free!"

CHAPTER V.

GETHSEMANE, OLIVET, AND BETHANY.

> " Sad Gethsemane
> Had memories that it faltered to repeat;
> Such as the strengthening angels marked, appalled,
> Finding no dialect in which to bear
> Their woe to heaven."

GETHSEMANE! What magic is there in the name! Who is not familiar with the sad story connected with its sacred soil? and who does not long to behold this place above all others?

It is now surrounded by a high wall; and a Romish monk guards the gate. As he silently turns the key, and admits us through the narrow doorway, what is our surprise on finding it converted into a modern flower garden! Rather attempt to gild refined gold, or add perfume to the violet, than endeavor to increase the interest of that spot by human art.

There are a few ancient olive trees, however (seven, I think), which are the only objects in keeping with the place. How affecting to sit beneath them, and read the account of the night of Christ's agony! Our hearts bleed as the incidents of the night of sorrow are vividly brought before us by the thrilling narrative. We linger and yet linger on the hallowed ground, and read and read again of the sufferings of our adorable Redeemer; we realize, that with the closing of the door of the Garden, the whole world has been shut out from our thoughts, leaving us in close communion with Jesus, the Divine sufferer. What Christian heart would remain indifferent to such associations! and who would not gladly brave the toil and danger of voyaging to this land for the sake of a seat beneath these venerable old silver-leafed olive trees!

" The Palm—the Vine—the Cedar—each hath power ;
    But thou, pale Olive ! in thy branches lie
    Far deeper spells than prophet grove of old
    Might e'er enshrine :—I could not hear thee sigh
    To the winds' faintest whisper, nor behold
    One shiver of thy leaves' dim silvery green,
    Without high thoughts and solemn, of that scene
    When, in the garden, the Redeemer prayed—
    When pale stars looked upon his fainting head.
 . And angels ministering in silent dread,
    Trembled, perchance, within *thy* trembling shade."

After culling a few flowers, whose fragrant
leaves are intended for distribution among
friends at home, we again call upon the monk
to turn his rusty key, and commence the
ascent of Mount Olivet, taking the road that
leads to the Church of Ascension. Here we
are shown the impress of a foot and staff in
the solid rock, which the credulous pilgrim is
told were made by Christ when about to ascend
on high. Around the Church, clusters a little
village, inhabited by the shepherds and farm-
ers of the neighboring land. On an introduc-

10

tion to the kind old Sheikh, who is intrusted with the keys of the Church, we are glad to accept his offer to conduct us to the top of the minaret, which commands the best view of the hills round about Jerusalem, as well as Jerusalem itself. Our eyes feast upon the most interesting localities on earth. There, right before us, is the very spot where the Temple stood, now desecrated by a Mohammedan mosque, of a thousand hues, and sky-piercing crescent. Next in prominence are the clumsy, massive domes of the Church of the Holy Sepulchre, and far beyond is the ever visible Tower of Hippicus.

To the left stretches out the wilderness of Judea; and, far in the distance, a silvery line and sparkling flat surface, denote the Jordan and Dead Sea. In the whole scene there is nothing to remind us of the western world; instead of tall forests, rapidly moving vehicles, and houses with pointed roofs, which would form the landscape in the new world, we see a few scattering trees of insignificant height, the slow-treading camel, and houses with flat roofs and hemispheric domes.

Jerusalem has the appearance of an immense cemetery; though it was once a city of palaces, we now behold a mass of ruins. Mount Zion, that was once covered with stately buildings, is now "ploughed like a field." Descending from the minaret, we pass through a group of mud huts, mostly composing the village, and enter the narrow path leading to Bethany.

The distance between Jerusalem and Bethany, is about two miles. It lies buried among the spurs of Mount Olivet, and is called by the Arabs "Lazareah" (the Lazarus). On the arrival of a traveller, an Arab lights a taper, and leads him down a few steps into a dark cave, said to be the tomb of Lazarus—the scene of one of Christ's greatest miracles.

Lazarus lay on a bed of sickness, and languishes from day to day, until his wan cheek shows that the hour of his departure is near

at hand.   The prayers of a fond sister are
hourly poured forth that help may come from
the arm, ever ready to extend relief alike to
friend and foe—and yet Jesus comes not.
Weary of the painful suspense, Mary and Martha send to Jesus, saying, "Lord, he whom
thou lovest is sick;" and his love for Lazarus
constrains him once more to visit Judea.

> " One grief, one faith, O, sisters of the dead !
>   Was in your bosoms—there whose steps made fleet
>   By keen hope fluttering in the heart which bled,
>   Bore thee as wings, the Lord of Life to greet ;
>   And thou, that duteous in thy still retreat
>   Didst wait his summons, then with reverent love
>   Fall weeping at the blest Deliverer's feet,
>   Whom e'en to heavenly tears thy woe could move :
>   And which to Him the All Seeing and All Just,
>   Was loveliest, that quick zeal, or lowly trust ?"

The death of Lazarus awakens in our Saviour the tenderest pity, and he weeps over his
grave.   But he no longer delays the happy
event that will turn this heaviness into joy.

He commands them to remove the stone that covered the mouth of the cave. Then, with a voice of Divine authority, he cries, "Lazarus, come forth!" Lo, the voice of Jesus awakens him from the sleep of death, and he comes forth, with aid from no other source, before the eyes of the astonished multitude. With what joy is he received from his grave by Mary and Martha, and what amazement stamps the face of every beholder!

We now resume the deeply worn path leading from Bethany to Jerusalem. Are we alone? No; Christ, who so often wandered over these hills, walks at our side — for these scenes most vividly recall the incidents of his life, and the very words that he spake — even this fig tree that grows at the side of our path reminds us of one of the lessons taught by our adorable Master — a lesson of faith, "whereunto we do well to take heed."

But, weary with walking and looking, every sense is now painfully conscious of fatigue, and

10 *

earnestly demands repose. Let us rest, then,
dear reader, upon this friendly rock beneath
the shade of the mulberry tree which bends
nearly to the ground.

To our right is the Chapel of the Prediction, built upon the rock on which Christ
is said to have stood when he cried, "Oh!
Jerusalem, Jerusalem, thou that killest the
prophets, and stonest them that are sent unto
thee, how often would I have gathered thy
children together, even as a hen gathereth
her chickens under her wings, and ye would
not! Behold, your house is left unto you desolate." Ah! He that spake as never man spake
uttered no prediction which has been more ter-
ribly fulfilled. See! there lies the "City of the
Great King" not more than half a mile from
our flinty divan—but how art thou fallen, O
Jerusalem! Is that little town of only twenty
thousand inhabitants, and not three miles in
circumference, all that is left of that mighty
city which was once "the joy of the whole

earth?"   Surely her glory is departed, for she is now but the neglected capital of a petty Turkish province!

While refreshing ourselves with these delicious mulberries, which grow here in such rich abundance, shall we glance at the history of the Holy City, as it passes in panoramic view before us, from the past, through the present, into the future?   Turn then to the west, and behold the Priest of the Most High (Melchisedec), who founds the city in the year of the world 2023, and calls it Salem; fifty years after which, it is captured by the descendants of Jebus, a son of Canaan, and receives the name of Jerusalem—*a vision of peace.*   In the year 597 B.C., Nebuchadnezzar overruns all Syria, enters Jerusalem, plunders the Temple, and carries away Daniel the prophet, and all the chief citizens, to Babylon.   But look! seventy years later may be seen these children of Israel returning to their beloved city, led by Ezra, their priest and scribe, who has been appointed governor by Cyrus. While peace yet continues, the books of the Old Testament are collected and arranged in their present form by Ezra, the walls are rebuilt by Nehemiah, and the Temple is partially restored. But now that restless, ambitious man of Macedon pours in his countless hordes upon this quiet people. During the year 333 B.C., he receives the submission of the city, and transplants one hundred thousand Jews to his Egyptian colony. Again and again is this doomed city pillaged and almost destroyed by the Ptolemies and the Persian kings.

Rome, in turn, becomes its conqueror, and holds the world in check while the most wonderful event occurs—"A child is born, upon whose shoulder the government shall rest; and his name shall be called Wonderful, Counsellor, The mighty God, The everlasting Father, The Prince of Peace; and of the increase of his government there shall be no end!" He lives a few years, during which time he accomplishes the greatest work ever witnessed by earth or Heaven—man's redemption—and dies an atonement for all our sin. How wonderful are the results! Asia and Africa are now open to receive his gospel, and the uttermost parts of earth his glad-tidings of great joy. Here is Christianity established, and from hence flows forth its blessing as a mighty river.

But now persecutions rage in the vain attempt to extinguish this Holy Light which has sprung up in a dark place—the city is doomed to destruction, and its people to dispersion. Titus is the instrument of wrath, and, during his siege, two hundred thousand Jews perish by famine. They had spilt the blood of Jesus, and cried, "His blood be upon us and our children." God answered their prayer, and chose for himself another people. Adrian follows Titus, and completes the work of destruction, and the name of the Jewish capital is changed and almost forgotten, until the idols erected upon the alleged sepulchre

of Christ are overthrown, and Constantine
once more establishes Christianity. But in
vain does Julian attempt to rebuild the Temple, for balls of fire are seen to issue from the
foundations, dispersing the laborers and pre-
venting their designs. Destined to endure
still further troubles, it struggles with Persia,
and passes under the Mohammedan yoke.

This is too grievous to be borne—the Holy
City governed by the Turk! This must not
be! To the rescue! Help! Christians, to the
rescue!! Shall the City of our King be thus
despised and trampled under foot? Ha! they
come! The voice of Peter the Hermit has
been heard! See there; Europe has sent her
chivalry—fair maidens and proud dames have
bidden their loved ones go and drive the Turk
from the Tomb of Christ. They come with
stout hearts and strong arms, and, headed by
the hermit Peter, and Godfrey de Bouillon,
besiege the town; and see, O joy! the standard of Christianity is waving on its walls!!

Alas! victory soon takes its flight—crusade follows crusade, and the city has many conquerors both Christian and Turk; and now the crescent displaces the cross, and the Moslem rule is still degrading this once noble and magnificent kingdom.

> "The Niobe of nations! there she stands,
>   Childless and crownless in her voiceless woe,
>   An empty urn within her withered hands,
>   Whose holy dust was scattered long ago."

The veil of the future is partly uplifted by the hand of prophecy, and, as we turn from the past, we see, coming from all directions, the Hebrew race—long scattered throughout the four quarters of the earth, yet still retaining their indelible national characteristics, and the same hope of returning to their ancient city, and of their own prosperity in the land of their forefathers.

Pollok, with almost prophetic eye and pen, portrays the scene in millennial strains:—

"How fair the daughter of Jerusalem then!
   How gloriously from Zion Hill she looked!
   Clothed with the sun, and in her train the moon,
   And on her head a coronet of stars,
   And girdling round her waist, with heavenly grace,
   The bow of mercy bright; and in her hand
   Immanuel's cross, her sceptre and her hope.

"Desire of every land! the nations came,
   And worshipped at her feet; all nations came,
   Flocking like doves: Columbia's painted tribes,
   That from Magellan to the frozen Bay,
   Beneath the Arctic, dwelt; and drank the tides
   Of Amazona, prince of earthly streams;
   Or slept at noon beneath the giant shade
   Of Andes' Mount; or roving northward, heard
   Niagara sing, from Erie's billow down
   To Frontenac, and hunted thence the fur
   To Labrador: and Afric's dusky swarms,
   That from Morocco to Angola dwelt,
   And drank the Niger from his native wells,
   Or roused the lion in Numidia's groves;
   The tribes that sat among the fabled cliffs
   Of Atlas, looking to Atlanta's waves,
   With joy and melody, arose and came.
   Zara awoke and came, and Egypt came,
   Casting her idol gods into the Nile.
   Black Ethiopia, that, shadowless,

Beneath the Torrid burned, arose and came.
Dauma and Medra, and the pirate tribes
Of Algeri, with incense came, and pure
Offerings, annoying now the seas no more.
The silken tribes of Asia, flocking, came,
Innumerous: Ishmael's wandering race, that rode
On camels o'er the spicy tract that lay
From Persia to the Red Sea coast; the King
Of broad Cathay, with numbers infinite,
Of many lettered casts; and all the tribes
That dwelt from Tigris to the Ganges' wave,
And worshipped fire, or Brahma, fabled God;
Cashmeres, Circassians, Banyans, tender race!
That swept the insect from their path, and lived
On herbs and fruits; and those who peaceful dwelt
Along the shady avenue that stretched
From Agra to Lahore; and all the hosts
That owned the crescent late, deluded long;
The Tartar hordes, that roamed from Oby's bank,
Ungoverned, southward to the wondrous Wall.
The tribes of Europe came: the Greek, redeemed
From Turkish thrall, the Spaniard came and Gaul,
And Britain with her ships; and, on his sledge,
The Laplander, that nightly watched the bear
Circling the pole; and those who saw the flames
Of Hecla burn the drifted snow; the Russ,
Long whiskered, and equestrian Pole; and those
Who drank the Rhine, or lost the evening sun

11

Behind the Alpine towers; and she that sat
By Arno, classic stream; Venice and Rome,
Head quarters long of sin! first guileless now,
And meaning as she seemed, stretched forth her hands;
And all the isles of ocean rose and came,
Whether they heard the roll of banished tides,
Antipodes to Albion's wave, or watched
The Moon, ascending chalky Teneriffe,
And with Atlanta holding nightly love.
The Sun, the Moon, the Constellations, came:
Thrice twelve and ten that watched the Antarctic sleep,
Twice six that near the Ecliptic dwelt, thrice twelve
And one that with the Streamers danced, and said
The Hyperborean ice guarding the Pole.
The East, the West, the South, and snowy North,
Rejoicing met and worshipped reverently
Before the Lord, in Zion's holy hill;
And all the places round about were blessed.

"The flocks and herds o'er hill and valley spread,
Exulting cropped the ever budding herb.
The desert blossomed and the barren sung;
Justice and mercy, holiness and love,
Among the people walked, Messiah reigned,
And Earth kept jubilee a thousand years.

But come; the curtain of night is falling.

and unless we reach the city ere the muezzim's cry, the gates will be closed against us.

As we enter the city his voice is heard, calling all good Mahommedans to prayer:—

> " Allah hoo ackbar—   Allah hoo ackbar,
> God is greater—   God is greater,
> Oo ishod la illa il Allah—
> And bear testimony to one God—
> Oo ishod la illa il Allah,
> And bear testimony to one God,
> Oo inne Mohommed el Resûl Allah.
> And testify that Mohammed is the Prophet of God."

Five times a day is this summons repeated— at mid-day, in the afternoon, at sunset, after dark, and, with this addition, at daybreak:—

> " Es Salat ophdel min en-nom.
> Prayer is better than sleep.
> Es Sullah koom wa kheddin es Salat.
> Rise up and offer Prayers."

CHAPTER VI.

A SUMMER ON MOUNT OLIVET.

> " Mount Olivet, in sighs,
> Spake mournfully—His midnight prayer was mine,
> I heard it, I alone,—as all night long
> Upward it rose with tears, for those who paid
> His love with hatred."

THE malaria arising from the debris of Jerusalem, compels all Frank residents, who wish to live out a full year, to pitch their tents in the country, and remain outside the walls several months of the warm season. Nothing is more primitive than this way of living. Families supply themselves with the mere necessaries of life, and occupy either tents or the ruins around the city. Never were we happier than when living in this way on the western spur of Mount Olivet, just opposite Jerusalem.

(124)

SUMMER RESIDENCE ON OLIVET, OVERLOOKING THE KEDRON

One is constantly reminded of the days of the Patriarchs. The surrounding hills abound in grapes, pomegranates, almonds, apricots, and figs; and these formed our principal articles of food. Some of our Bedawin friends brought us one day a bag of fruit from the neighborhood of the Jordan, which they affirm are the veritable apples of Sodom. They were beaten into a powder, and whether the apple of Sodom, or fruit of Gomorrah, it was very palatable. In exchange, they earnestly pleaded for the only looking-glass we had brought with us—of the size of one's hand. From the sensation it produced amongst them, it was evident they had never seen one before. The eyes of the women especially sparkled from very delight, on surveying its reflection of the beads, coins, and tassels with which their heads were decorated. This, together with an electrical machine, telescope, and the dispensary of medicines, drew great numbers of them to our abode. Scores of these sons of the desert

11 *

might be seen winding around the mountain every day, and a formidable company they were—each one mounted on his fine prancing charger, and armed with all manner of deadly instruments, a very walking battery. But, however wild their aspect, owing to the potent influence of medicine, we were always treated by them with the greatest kindness.

The profound ignorance of these semi-civilized beings, very naturally leads to the grossest superstition, of which we often had instances. Of medicinal knowledge, they have none—but substitute all kinds of foolish and superstitious practices in its stead. The application of the red-hot iron is one of their most popular remedies. A man fell one day from a house-top; a messenger was despatched on a fleet horse for a Frank physician, who found him dangerously wounded, and an Arab doctor applying a red-hot iron, which, in their full belief in its efficacy, afforded the greatest imaginable comfort to the unfortunate man, and to his sympa-

thizing friends!   At other times, the sick man
is laid near the tomb of some saint; or a golden
case, containing a verse from the Koran, is hung
around his neck.   Frequently a choice sentence
from the Koran is placed in a pipe and smoked,
and this they rely upon as a cure for the most
dangerous maladies!   Another popular mode
of treatment is a severe flogging!

When a paper of medicine is given them,
such is their ignorance, that they receive it
with the idea that both paper and medicine
must be swallowed!

During our first summer encampment, the
Pacha and his Hareem removed for the benefit
of their health to the village crowning the top
of the mountain.   Great was the excitement,
when the long train of white sheets and attendants were seen approaching the village.   Rooms
had been already overspread with costly di-
vans, and the villagers had arrayed themselves
in holiday attire for their reception.   Soon
after their arrival, as in etiquette bound, I

called to pay my respects. The queen of the hareem, who is a beautiful young Circassian, handed me her own elegant narghileh to smoke. I received many other marks of favor, and was frequently assured that my visit afforded them great pleasure.

They were not long in returning my visit; a messenger, however, was first sent, to say that the ladies earnestly requested the gentlemen to leave the house. (Curious ladies, these!) This was, of course, readily complied with, however reluctantly; and we endeavored to please our distinguished visitors. Some were not well, and wanted medicine, which we freely gave them, and they would fain have prostrated themselves in gratitude; indeed, it was sometimes a difficult task to prevent a patient from thus falling on the floor and kissing our feet. Ever after this they were frequent visitors at our encampment, notwithstanding its humble appearance; for it was a small, dilapidated house, with two rooms and a stable, so

constructed that the stable was the hall of
entrance. A tent was pitched near the door,
of rather greater pretensions, being highly decorated with figures of white and green. But
the privilege of living on this delightful mountain, so full of soul-stirring associations, and of
treading daily the path so often trodden by the
feet of our Saviour, fully compensated for the
trivial privations we endured. For

" Here with His flock the sad Wanderer came—
    These hills, He toil'd over in grief, are the same—
    The founts where he drank by the wayside still flow,
    And the same airs are blowing which breathed on his brow!"

Our simple manner of living gave additional
enjoyment; and to contribute our mite of good
by administering to the sick, as well as to scat-
ter " the leaves which are for the healing of
the nations;" and, with Bible in hand, to roam
over those sacred localities, were never-ending
sources of pleasure.

But one of the most attractive features of

this simple life is the vivid everyday repro-
duction of scriptural incidents.

How many passages are to be found in
which allusion is made to skin bottles, which
formed our most indispensable articles of
furniture! The use of these still prevails ex-
tensively throughout the East, and although
earthen jugs are also used, the former are
greatly preferred, and much more common.
They are made of the skin of a goat or a
sheep, and are so slightly mutilated by preparation for use, that they retain almost the
exact shape of the animal from which they
were made. They are hung on the back of a
donkey, or more frequently a woman, and,
having been filled with water, thousands are
carried daily to the city. Abraham provided
Hagar with a *bottle* of water on sending her to
the desert; but, properly rendered, might it not
be *water-skin?* They are sometimes regularly
tanned into leather. This was no doubt the
material of the wine-bottles of the Gibeonitish

WOMAN WITH WATER-SKIN.   TURKISH SOLDIER.   ARAB SPINNING.

spies, who "did work wilily, and went and made as if they had been ambassadors, and took old sacks upon their asses, and wine-bottles old and rent, bound up." These bottles, from constant use, become rent, and when mended and patched give full proof of good service and an ancient date. Hence, to put new wine in these old bottles would be utter folly, for the process of fermentation would cause them to "break through," which would not be the case while new and flexible.

Our camping-ground being very near the well that supplies the village with water, I often met the village maidens there, who repaired thither to fill their jugs. Their usual time for drawing water is just before nightfall, and the office is always performed by the women, as in the days of the Patriarchs; for we read that Eleazar, whom Abraham had sent to obtain a wife for Isaac, made his camels to kneel down without the city by a well of water at the time of the evening, even the time that women go out to draw water. And Rebekah, the very maiden whom he sought, "came out with her pitcher upon her shoulder, and she went down to the well and filled her pitcher and came up." How often have I called upon fancy to imagine the retreating form of a Fellahah, with a vessel on her head or shoulder, and decorated with bracelets and ear-rings, to be the veritable Rebekah of old !

A stone trough is generally placed near the well, from which cattle are watered, and around it a flock of goats or sheep is usually gathered, as in the days of Jacob, who beheld a well in the field, and "three flocks of sheep lying by it." And in another particular they agree with the wells of the days of the Patriarchs, in having the mouth covered with a large stone of great weight, requiring the strength of two men sometimes to move it. The usual method of drawing water is with a jug or leathern bucket, let down by a rope tied to its mouth; and when the well has been long in use, deep incisions are made by the rope in the topmost lining stones. This method was no doubt referred to by the woman at the Well of Samaria, when she said, "The well is deep, and I have nothing to draw with." It is also seen from Gen. xxix. 8, that the present manner of covering the well is the same as that which made it necessary for Rachel to require the greater strength of Jacob to roll the stone away, when she came to water the flocks of her father.

Among all orientals, even these simple Fellahin, dress is a matter of great importance, and they have a passionate fondness for ornaments. A poor Fellah, with a mud hut for his dwelling, and bread and water, literally, for his food (varied now and then with a cucumber), decorates the head of his child with gold and silver coins, which nothing less than the prospect of starvation would induce him to devote to other purposes. The women,

12

too, wear this heavy head-gear, from which a veil of coarse white cloth hangs over the shoulder. The remainder of the dress is nothing more than a blue gown, with sleeves reaching to the ground, and a girdle around the waist. We are always made aware of their approach by the tinkling anklets, brace-lets, and head ornaments.

The dress of the men is equally simple, consisting of a white tunic bound around the loins with a leathern girdle, a turban, and sometimes an outer garment of coarse material, striped, brown, and white, serving the double purpose of an article of apparel and a bed. And this enables us to under-stand the mysterious command of Christ to the sick man, to whom he said, after curing him of his disease, "Take up thy bed and walk." The dress of the Bedaweh differs but little from that of the Fellahah, but we may always distinguish the former by her tattooed face and nose-ring. Neither is there any dif-

ference between that of the men, except that
the Bedawin wears a gay striped handkerchief
of yellow and crimson bound around his head
with a cord, while the Fellah merely wears a
turban.

Our summer on Mount Olivet passed rapidly
away, but the emotions which there thronged
upon my soul will never be forgotten. Often
did I realize that I stood on "Holy Land," and
my heart went out in communion with the
"mighty dead." There, in that very path-
way, leading directly from the city to Jordan,
by way of Bahurim, David went up, weeping
as he fled from his vile rebellious son, and
looking back with wistful eye on his beloved
capital, worshipped at an oratory just there,
near our ruined castle. Up that path yonder
by Gethsemane, "David's greater Son," our
adorable Redeemer, often toiled at the close of
the day, as he left the heaven-abandoned city,
to seek repose in Bethany. 'Twas on this
mountain that the Shekinah lingered when it

left the Temple! Yonder, on that conical summit, the last conference was held with the Apostles, as the Son of man was parted from them, and ascended on high, leading captivity captive. And upon this same hallowed mountain will his feet stand in "that day" when he shall come to be admired of his saints, and to take vengeance on his enemies. Sometimes I envied the old trees which afforded shade for the Saviour and the Apostles, and the breezes, those "children of eternity," which refreshed them after the toils and dangers of the day. Often did I interrogate them, and all the mountains round about Jerusalem : What know ye of my Saviour, the Son of God? and my heart hushed its noisy throbbing when I heard

> "Judea's mountains from their breezy heights
> Reply,—'We heard him, when he lifted up
> His voice, and taught the people patiently,
> Line upon line, for they were slow of heart.'
> From its dark depths, the Galilean lake
> Told hoarsely to the storm-cloud, how he dealt

Bread to the famished throng, with tender care,
Forgetting not the body, while he fed
The immortal spirit;—how he stood and healed,
Day after day, till evening shadows fell
Around the pale and paralytic train,
Lame, halt, and blind, and lunatic, who sought
His pitying touch."

　　　　　" Even Calvary,
Pressed close its flinty lip, and shuddering bowed
In silent dread, remembering how the sun
Grew dark at noonday, and the sheeted dead
Came from their cleaving sepulchres, to walk
Among the living."

12 *

CHAPTER VII.

VISIT TO THE JORDAN AND THE DEAD SEA.

It is considered unsafe to make the trip to the Jordan and the Dead Sea without a guard, and even then, one is in danger of "falling among thieves" and murderers of the most desperate kind—the merciless Bedawin, "whose hand is against every man." All our fears and misgivings, however, are dispelled on the arrival of the guard, who are sufficiently warlike in appearance to quell the fears of the most timid. Crossing the Valley of Jehosaphat, and then Mount Olivet, and passing the now palmless Bethany, and the Apostles' Fountain, we soon enter upon a waste so dreary, so entirely bereft of one spot of verdure, that it completely fulfils the idea conveyed by the word "wilderness."

Who would not at once recognise in this wide-spreading desert, the Wilderness of Judea? what a wild and fearful aspect it presents!

> " Here rocks alone, and ceaseless sands are found,
>   And faint and sickly winds for ever howl around."

It was on one of these barren hills, or in one of these dark ravines, that the good Samaritan attended so faithfully to the wounded Jew, whom the thieves had left in such a deplorable condition. On one of these towering mountains, Mount Quarantina, the Saviour was tempted for forty days and forty nights.

Rejoiced are we when our fatiguing ride, along the sides of the steep and craggy mountains, is ended at the banks of the Dead Sea, which we find just as mysterious as we have been led to expect by the accounts of travellers. The taste of the water is pungent and bitter, and its buoyancy so great, that one can float along with head and shoulders above water; and with a log of wood for a pillow, could leisurely read a newspaper. To sink is impossible—for, as Josephus well remarks, "no one was ever yet drowned in the Dead Sea."

Its surface is many hundred feet below that of the Mediterranean Sea, and at different seasons its level varies from ten to fifteen feet, the evaporation being very great. A few fresh-water streams flow into it, and the fish which are thus brought in are strangled in its briny waters, and float dead upon the surface. Recent analysis gives us, in one hundred grains of this water, twenty-five of salts, principally of soda and magnesia—while the water of the ocean has only ten. Being already saturated, common salt will not dissolve in it, and it is said to preserve vegetable and animal substances from decay. At its southern extremity is a ridge of rock salt, from one hundred to one hundred and fifty feet high, and nearly five miles long. The Arabs tell us that Lot's wife may be found here transformed into a pillar of salt, and point out a column of crystallized rock-salt, sixty feet high and forty in circumference, a lasting monument of female disobedience and improper indulgence in that characteristic trait of our sex—curiosity.   But we cannot believe all that these Arabs say, for they too often indulge in exaggerations, and delight in pointing out localities and objects which exist only in their imaginations.

About nightfall we reach Jericho, and pass the dreariest of nights within the walls of its filthy dilapidated castle.   The city of palms was long since destroyed—its site is now marked by this ancient tower, a few mud huts, and heaps of rubbish.   How deplorable the change, and complete the desolation following the curse of an offended God!   Who would remain unmoved on ground to which such interest attaches, as that of this memorable spot? It was in this vicinity that the children of Israel first entered the promised land.   On these craggy mountains the hosts of Israel were encamped, when their leader commanded them to possess themselves of the promised land : " Go over, thou and all this people, into the land which I do give thee, even the children of Israel." How melancholy to see the direful change caused by the backslidings and disobedience of this people!

After passing over this ground, the first object of note is the Fountain of Elisha, whose bitter waters the prophet miraculously made sweet. A few miles more terminates our ride, and brings us to the Jordan. In common with every traveller, we are disappointed on seeing its narrow muddy stream. We alight at the very spot handed down by tradition as the place of Christ's baptism—a retired part of the stream, bordered with tall luxuriant shrubbery and a few scattered trees.

On these banks were assembled the vast concourse of people attending the Forerunner's preaching; and He who knew no sin must needs also be baptized of him—an honor which John, in his humility and reverence for Christ, was loth to accept. But a word only was needed from his Master to gain his consent. On hearing the words, "Suffer it to be so now, for thus it becometh us to fulfil all righteousness," he baptized him; and, when they emerged from the water, "Lo, a voice from Heaven, This is my beloved Son, in whom I am well pleased;" and the eternal Spirit descended upon His sacred head. Hard, indeed, do we find it to realize that we are standing on ground memorized by so glorious a spectacle! But alas! how different now!

> " On Jordan's banks the Arab's camels stray,
>   On Sion's hill the False One's votaries pray,
>   The Baal-adorer bows on Sinai's steep—
>   Yet there—even there—Oh, God! thy thunders sleep.
>
>   There—where thy finger scorched the tablet stone!
>   There—where thy shadow to the people shone,
>   Thy glory shrouded in its garb of fire:
>   Thyself none living see and not expire!
>
>   Oh! in the lightning let thy glance appear!
>   Sweep from his shivered hand the oppressor's spear:
>   How long by tyrants shall thy land be trod!
>   How long thy temple worshipless, Oh, God!"

The rainy season having now commenced, we must leave our rustic abode for our city residence on Mount Zion, which we do with extreme reluctance, unwilling to exchange our rural encampment and pleasant walks for the more confined air, and the greater restraint of a walled city. But we are consoled with the knowledge that person and property are less exposed to the wandering tribes of Bedawin Arabs from beyond the Jordan, and are free from the snakes and scorpions which are so numerous on Mount Olivet.

The English and Germans, who have been spending the summer in tents outside the walls, have been compelled to beat a precipitate retreat into the city on account of the petty wars between the various tribes of Arabs in this vicinity; and we had, sometime ago, held a council with the chief men of Jebel Tûr (village of Ascension), who are also at war, as to the propriety of remaining any longer in our exposed position; but had determined to run

the hazard of a longer abode, on receiving
their solemn assurance that, if we were to
walk up that valley between them and the Isa-
weians, with whom they expected there to
fight, the next day, all firing would cease! So
much for the potent influence of medicine, and
their reverence for the Hakeem, or Physician!

13

CHAPTER VIII.

BETHLEHEM.

CORSICA was the birthplace of Napoleon, Eisleben of Luther, and Virginia of Washington; but when these are forgotten, Bethlehem will be remembered, and the multitude of holy associations which come thronging in upon the soul at the mention of that name, will never cease to be cherished with reverential memories in the inner sanctuary of the heart. France still worships at the shrine of Bonaparte; and those nations who felt his power have not forgotten that mighty man of war. Christendom still throbs with the energy infused into its sluggish heart by the courage and vigor of the monk of Saxony; and the civilized world has not ceased to wonder at the glorious results

BETHLEHEM.

which followed the labors of the patriot soldier
and Christian statesman, whose remains are now
mingled with Mount Vernon's dust; but the
world, and heaven, and hell, have been shaken
to the centre by the Babe born in a manger;
and thou, oh Bethlehem! art exalted above all
the earth, as the cradle of Divinity—the birthplace of a God! " Thou, Bethlehem Ephrata,
though thou be little among the thousands of
Judah, yet out of thee shall he come forth unto
me that is to be ruler in Israel; whose goings
forth have been from of old, from everlasting."

The road from Jerusalem to Bethlehem is
rough and stony, with the exception of the
Plain of Rephaim; and there is scarcely any
cultivation to be seen, save the terraced hill-
sides, which are planted with vineyards. But
the oriental traveller is accustomed to rough
roads, and rough roads only; with a good horse,
or a fleet little donkey, the ride of six miles is
soon over—that is, in an hour and a half—
which is considered rapid travelling in a land

where cars, steamboats, or wheeled vehicles of any kind are unknown.

The town stands on a hill, and presents a fine appearance from a distance; but an entrance soon convinces one that it is but little better than other oriental towns. The Church and Monastery, however, covering the Cave of the Nativity, are very imposing, and the interior contains much to boast of, among which is a long double row of elegant Corinthian pillars. The Cave of the Nativity is lighted by thirty lamps, which burn night and day, blinding the eye with their brilliancy; which, together with their reflection in the polished surfaces of the marble walls, completely bewilder one on first entering. The altars are continually wreathed with fragrant, freshly gathered flowers, and a silver star inserted in the floor, marks, it is said, the exact spot of our Saviour's birth. This may not be the true manger, as alleged, but at any rate it cannot be very far off. We will therefore satisfy ourselves with the belief that we are at least *near* the spot over which the star appeared, announcing the birth of the Messiah. In rapid succession, its incidents crowd upon the memory — the appearance of the star to a company of shepherds watching their flocks by night on these plains, and also to the wise men who go to Bethlehem to worship the babe, and pour out their offerings of gold, frankincense, and myrrh; the unavailing efforts of Herod to destroy the child; and the flight of Mary and Joseph with their precious charge into Egypt.

The shepherds saw the star, and knew its meaning; full of joy and wonder, they publish abroad the glad tidings. With haste they go to Bethlehem, leaving their flocks, as things of no value, compared with the blissful sight awaiting them. They are directed by the angels; and remembering the word of prophecy in relation to the wonderful babe, they go to Bethlehem. There they ask, " Where is he that is born King of the Jews?" On discover-

13 *

ing the lowly place of his birth, they fall down and worship him.

Herod is troubled at the startling account of the birth of our Saviour, and seeks to kill the child, but in vain. The tyrant sends wise men to Bethlehem in search of the new-born king. They look in vain for a princely abode; and great is their wonder on beholding the group before them : Christ, in the manger, Mary his mother, and Joseph her betrothed husband, in garments becoming their humble estate. But their adoration is not withheld, notwithstanding the great disappointment in their hopes and expectations. Wonderingly they fall down and worship him, and humbly present their costly offerings. Herod little dreams that his evil machinations are to meet with no success ; but so it had been ordained of Divine Wisdom. The babe lives, notwithstanding his wicked designs.

Before leaving Bethlehem, we visit the school-room of the estimable and devoted Miss Williams, and find her engaged in teaching a group of bright-looking Arab children, who progress rapidly under their experienced and indefatigable teacher.

One of the most absurd of all the ceremonies performed at the Church of the Nativity, is the exorcism of evil spirits. Smile not, for it is even so! A high ecclesiastical dignitary of the Church of Rome—no less a personage than the Patriarch of Jerusalem—assisted by a long retinue of Bishops and other clergy in full canonicals, annually performs this solemn mockery a few days before the Latin Christmas—for you must know that they have two or three Christmases at Bethlehem! Some of our party who witnessed this droll mummery were unable to restrain their risibles at sight of the curious and violent gesticulations of these reverendissimos, when they would apparently corner one of the demons and cast him out of the church. But, though we had not intentionally offended them, our want of faith in

their exorcising powers well nigh cost us a
night's lodging in prison. Having never witnessed the grand ceremonies of "Christi Missa,"
we visited Bethlehem one Friday evening for
the purpose of attending them. We repaired
to the Church of the Nativity at eight o'clock,
and remained seated for some time in perfect
silence, when the Latin Patriarch of Jerusalem
approached us, and inquired, through a priest
who spoke imperfect English, whether we were
Catholics? "Yes," was the reply, "we are
Bible Christians, and, of course, Catholics."
"And do you believe in the real presence?"
continued the heretic-detector. "We believe
that the Divine Redeemer is everywhere present," said father, not being aware that the
question was asked with special reference to
the services upon which they were about to
engage. A long discussion ensued relative to
the "*real presence;*" and when we informed
him that we were not Roman Catholics, he
insisted upon our immediate departure. On

observing a manifest reluctance on our part, he terminated the conversation and shouted, "Jeeb Kawass;" which, being interpreted, means "bring the janizaries;" and forthwith several subalterns hastened off to summon them. Anxious to avoid all difficulties, we retreated to the Church of St. Helena, owned by the Armenians, where we were heartily welcomed and assured of protection by sympathizing friends who had witnessed our expulsion. But we soon discovered that even here we were kept under strict surveillance, and continued our walk to the reputed sites of Jerome's Cave, Joseph's house, and the manger. Soon after descending into the Grotto of the Nativity, we received a message from *his grace*, who wished to visit the Star and the Manger, and desired us to depart. Being fully assured, however, that here at least we had a right to remain as long as the church was open, we were slow to take our departure; but on refusing to kneel to the uplifted wafer, the officiating priest commanded our expulsion, and raised the cry of "Brotestanti." Forthwith the vaulted archways rang with loud cries of "Protestant! Protestant! Protestant!" and in less time than is required to describe the scene, we were forcibly expelled from the premises.

CHAPTER IX.

EXCURSIONS TO WADY FARAH AND LIFTAH.

THE sun was gilding the tops of the olive trees on Mount Olivet when we passed the Church of Ascension on our way to Wady Farah—one of the most lovely spots in all the neighborhood of the Holy City. Merrily we cantered over the hills in the fresh morning air,—father and brother mounted on their prancing steeds, myself seated on my little donkey, while faithful Mahmoud, well armed, and our dog, made up our little party. And here it behooves me to pay a passing tribute to "Pharaoh Necho," the prince of donkeys, and "Dickens," the noblest of the canine race. Struck with the many marks of beauty exhibited in Pharaoh Necho's form, a Russian

(155)

nobleman had selected him from a choice lot
arrayed for his inspection while at Cairo. On
reaching Jerusalem, having no further use for
him, he offered him for sale at the low price
of four hundred piastres, assuring us that he
had kept before the caravan throughout the
journey from Cairo to Jerusalem through the
long desert. Of course the temptation to purchase him was irresistible. Every one congratulated me on my good fortune, and said
there had never been seen such a donkey in
the streets of Jerusalem. Right proudly did I
mount him, when, shortly after the purchase,
he was brought to me saddled and bridled for
my first ride. He was mouse-colored, his skin
soft and glossy; his limbs delicately and ex-
quisitely formed, and striped à la zebra. Ac-
coutred in true Arab style, with a crimson saddle cloth, gayly adorned with tinsel, and bridle
hung with every species of oriental paraphernalia, he never failed to strike every one with
the most profound admiration; and the little

boys who came in his way with his hind feet!
He has been known to whip three camels in a
fair fight; and was justly called a hyena for his
ferocity. As for his gait, it was compared by
the Arabs to the swiftness of the wind! The
donkey and the dog were inseparable; and the
enjoyment of a ride was never considered complete by any party concerned, without the
barking of the dog, harmoniously blended with
the braying of the donkey! The sagacity of
"Dickens" justly merits a word of praise. He
exhibited a limited knowledge of the Arabic
language, and was quite accomplished in the
art of singing. Now, while Monsieur Dickens
was, of course, unable to express himself in
words, he showed that he perfectly understood
us whenever an order was given to saddle the
donkey, by the most frantic demonstrations of
delight; and such was his passion for music,
that whenever he heard the sound of the gui-
tar or accordeon, he would immediately discover my whereabouts; and if at first I refused

14

admittance, his piteous moans would soon induce me to open the door; and while resting his head in my lap, he would accompany the instrument without making a discordant note; on the contrary, his voice was quite musical, and wonderfully like that of a human being.

On several occasions, when we expelled him from our little chapel, he found his way to the top of an opposite house, from whence he could hear our hymns, and unite his voice with ours. But Dickens, though a wonderful dog, had one serious fault, which was his great antipathy to the Jews. On the approach of an Israelite, meanly clad, his custom was to jump upon him, and, forcing him to the ground, leave him unhurt, though badly frightened. He was, however, very polite to Turks and Christians.

Following our rocky path a short distance beyond Mount Olivet, we made a detour to a fountain, of which marvellous accounts were afloat. Our guide here pretended to call the water forth from the ground, and in a few minutes cause it again to subside, by repeating a mysteriously worded chant. Sure enough, on singing a long incantation, of which the chorus was, " the colored man whipped the white man," the water immediately gushed forth; and allowing a little while to elapse, he reversed the chorus, and the water disappeared beneath the ground. By remaining on the spot a short time, however, we discovered it was one of the wonders of nature, instead of a miraculous display of human power; and had we remained days on the spot, the stream would have continued to appear and disappear at regular intervals. Returning to the path, we descended with the greatest difficulty the steep, precipitous route to Wady Farah, or the " Valley of Delight," for such is the signification of the name. We were often compelled to dismount and walk—to remain in the saddle being dangerous both to rider and beast. The last hill that hid the lovely Eden from our view was now safely passed, and I fully realized the high expectations that had been raised by the glowing description given me by my father and brothers, who had already visited it several times. Their last visit, however, gave occasion for anything but pleasant recollections of the place—for they were shot at by the fierce Arabs, who frequent the caves in the sides of the hills, and were obliged to flee for their lives. The cause of this savage treatment was my father's purchase of the valley; and the Arabs, supposing that the Frank intruders had come to take possession of the place, adopted this method of showing their decided unwillingness to share with them their paradisaic rendezvous.

One of the offenders having been caught, and subjected to a long imprisonment, was sent to beg their pardon, and kiss their feet. But he was readily pardoned, such abject humiliation not being required. Quiet having been

restored by the good old Pacha, we entertained
no fear of a second adventure.

Nothing could have been more peaceful than
the aspect of the valley when we entered it,
and listened with charmed senses to the chirp-
ing of the birds, and the musical gurgling of
the water which coursed the valley, now empty-
ing itself into a marble basin, and now retreating beneath a hiding-place of luxuriant clusters
of shrubbery. As for its other occupants, there
was nothing in them calculated to inspire the
most timid with emotions even approaching to
fear, for its sole tenants, besides the birds, were
a few conies climbing the rocks, some Arab
women filling their skins with water, and
quantities of tiny fish sporting in the basins;
while the graceful form of a gazelle might occasionally be seen disappearing behind a hill-top
in the distance. The basins of fish, as well as
a few remains of masonry, and some ancient
coins, we could account for in no other way
than to conjecture that they were the remains

14 *

of improvements made by the crusaders, who on discovering this lovely retreat employed the chisel and hammer, as well to increase its attractiveness as to render useful the advantages so bountifully bestowed by the hand of nature. On either side of the valley are towering ledges of rock, in which rooms have been hewn, at least as far back as the days of the crusaders, for the purpose of affording safe retreats in time of danger. They can only be reached by means of a long ladder, which was afterwards procured, carried down there, and such of the rooms as could be reached were explored. At the upper end of the valley is an amphitheatrical cave, of such immense size and height that I never experienced greater awe than that inspired by this grand old church, sculptured and fashioned by the hand of nature, or in other words, by the hand of the great Jehovah. From the location of this valley it is thought to be " Enon near to Salim, where John was baptizing because there was much water there;" for it is not only near a ruined city, and a valley called Salem by the Arabs to this day, but corresponds in every other particular with the Scripture narrative.

A short time after our visit to this place we rode out to another interesting locality, seldom visited by travellers, yet identified with the Nephtoah of the Bible, though pronounced by the Arabs Liftah. It is a copious fountain situated about two miles from Jerusalem, so cool, shady, and inviting, in every respect, that the Anglican Bishop has selected a hill in its immediate vicinity, for his camping-ground during the summer. Soon after seating myself to take a sketch of the place, long lines of well armed Arabs were seen descending the hills, causing us some doubt and perplexity as to the meaning of the visit, not unmixed with fear at the approach of such a formidable train. We endeavored however to converse with them in an unfaltering tone, and preserve a careless air; for nothing is more important among the

Arabs than an outward show of bravery, whatever be the misgivings within. Many were the suspicious glances directed toward us, but on learning that the Frank gentleman was a Hakeem, their manner changed, and many of them eagerly gathered around him to have their pulses felt and tongues examined; and seemed delighted to hear that he would give them medicine, if they would come to his "hackmè" in the city. I noticed that every one paid great respect to a stately but scowling chieftain, who sat under a tree surrounded by attendants with folded arms and heads bowed down; but we could not ascertain his name. Deeming it unsafe to remain longer among this wild terror-inspiring tribe, we gladly took our departure with an unfinished sketch; and when safely mounted on my donkey, I did not once venture to look behind lest I should see them in close pursuit. A deputation of peacemakers, despatched by the Pacha of Damascus, had just arrived, and it is probable that we owed our escape in no small measure to that fortunate circumstance. The next day we were told, by one of the party who came in for medical advice, that the chieftain was no less a personage than Abu Gosh, the celebrated robber and murderer. He had conducted his forces thither for the purpose of having a pitched battle the following day with the tribe of Leham,—the two tribes having long been at enmity with each other; and we were warned for "Allah's" sake never to venture again so far from the walls during those troublous times. The neighboring country was convulsed with petty wars, and murders were an every-day occurrence— a Turkish officer even, having been openly robbed and murdered, within sight and range of the battery of the citadel.

CHAPTER X.

VISIT TO THE MOSQUE OF OMAR.

I WAS as much surprised as delighted one day on receiving a polite invitation, from some of my Turkish friends, to assume their disguising mantle, and accompany them to the Mosque of Omar. I could hardly believe it possible that I was about to enjoy the privilege of walking on the hallowed ground of the Temple enclosure, of standing beneath its mournful cypresses, and setting foot on the site of the Holy of Holies itself; nor did I succeed in convincing myself that I was not dreaming, until fully equipped in their curious and most unmanageable costume. The transformation was complete. Ten minutes before, in my simple American dress, and now rigged

(166)

VIEW OF HAREM ES SHERIF FROM CHURCH OF ST. ANNE.

MOSK OF OMAR.

)ut so perfectly à la Turk, that my own nother would not have recognised me! My friends were greatly amused and delighted. The slippers gave me the most trouble; and I was heartily laughed at whenever I attempted to walk. The peculiar shuffling gait of oriental women must be learned, as an additional safeguard against detection; and great was the mirth I excited at every attempt to hobble across the room, which the enormous size of the slippers made it almost impossible to do. How should I get along in the street? was a query that gave rise to many fears and misgivings. The slippers I feared would certainly drop off, and the veil I felt sure would smother me; for, besides being very thick, it was closely wrapped round my face.

My costume consisted of full silk trousers, a trailing robe whose ends were securely tucked within my girdle, an embroidered vest, large yellow morocco boots, and over them slippers of the same material, turned up at the toes like a skate. A red fez cap was placed on my head, and around it a gauze turban edged with a fringe work of balls of gold. Over my whole person a white sheet was thrown, which required quite as much attention as the slippers; and although every precaution was taken, and innumerable pins brought into requisition for its security, it was not until I had gone through a severe process of drilling that I learnt rightly to manage my ghostly outer garb. My veil, though thick, was fortunately of such a texture that I could dimly see those around me, though my own features could not be distinguished. Next, I was warned that a word would betray me, and therefore I must preserve perfect silence, leaving the talking to them. To give the greater force to this injunction, they placed their forefingers on their mouths, and remained mute for some moments themselves, thus impressing it by example as well as precept.

On descending the steps, new difficulties

awaited me in the way of keeping on my slippers, which increased the merriment of my companions tenfold, affording proof that these poor creatures do know how to laugh—a fact hard to be credited when we think of their lifetime of slavish imprisonment! At a short distance there was a group of Effendis, and as I passed them I had many misgivings about my unwieldy wrappings; but a close observance of the directions I received before sallying forth, enabled me to retain them, and the lordly Turk was for once outwitted by the despised "Infidel!" My prospects were brightening, and I felt encouraged. At the gate we encountered the jetty Nubians who guard the Haram, and I shuddered as I glanced at their fierce countenances and terror-inspiring clubs. But I congratulated myself that they too were quite unconscious of the concealment of an "infidel dog" beneath the folds of one of those white sheets, else I had met with perhaps worse treatment than that awarded the English

15

doctor a short time before. On venturing barely within the precincts of the enclosure, to visit a patient who occupied a house near one of the gates, he was knocked down from his horse by a score of these ferocious fellows, dreadfully beaten, and for a length of time was confined to his room from the wounds inflicted by their nail-pierced clubs—indeed it was nearly the occasion of his death.

Having passed them I breathed freely—that is, as much so as my provoking veil would allow me—and was again complacently congratulating myself, when my inward boastings were suddenly put to flight, by the consciousness that I had lost a slipper; and, in stooping to replace it, my veil dropped, disclosing my face to several acquaintances standing just in front of us! They would no doubt have recognised me, had they not immediately turned their backs—a custom always observed by the men on meeting females, for fear of committing the grievous sin of seeing a woman's face.

The non-observance of this act is thought exceedingly rude; and, fortunately for me, it was on this occasion strictly adhered to.

Ascending a wide flight of stone steps, we passed an elegant Saracenic portal, and gained the marble-paved platform from the centre of which rises the towering Mosque of Omar. The sun was shining brightly on the variously colored porcelain with which it is covered in intricate patterns, and reflected all around the rainbow hues of the fifty-six windows with which it is pierced; and the cypress trees waved gracefully over the pretty little praying-places scattered here and there on the green· grass. Indeed it seemed to me fairy land, and I was reminded at every step of the marvellous stories of the "Arabian Nights' Entertainments." The dome of the Mosque is said to be the most symmetrical in the world, and the whole is thought to be unsurpassed in grace and beauty.

The platform being considered very holy, we

doffed our slippers, and gave them in charge to an attendant slave; a very ancient practice, for we learn from the Old Testament that the Jewish priests always removed their shoes on entering the Temple, and never officiated except in their bare feet; and this practice was, on one occasion, a direct command from Jehovah; for we are told that Moses was divinely warned to put off his shoes on the miraculous appearance of the burning bush. Such is the importance still attached to this custom by eastern nations, that they are struck with holy horror and greatly incensed when the unscrupulous traveller attempts to pollute their churches and mosques with shod feet; and on entering places like this esteemed especially holy, a compliance with the rule is absolutely required. At this moment, hearing footsteps of persons behind us, we turned in another direction to avoid them, and strolled leisurely to the Mosque of Aksa, passing an exquisite pulpit and fountain of variegated marble. By the pulpit is an elaborate urn, and overhanging it a cluster of cypress, olive, and acacia trees, forming a most enchanting little spot. I lingered here, intent on gathering flowers as mementoes of the place, until warned by a sudden jerk at my sheet, of the approach of a Derwish.

In El-Aksa, seeing no one near, I ventured to raise my veil, in order to enjoy the luxury of fresh air; but it was no sooner raised than pulled down again by my companion, accompanied by the same significant pressure of her forefinger on her lips. On looking up to discover the cause of so unwelcome an intrusion upon the comfort of my respiratory organs, whom should I see but the same old Derwish, bearing an antique-shaped jug and bunch of keys, indicative of his office, as keeper of the holy places. This curious building is hardly describable. The exterior presents very much the appearance of a barn, with a dome at one end, and a row of pillars and arches at the

15 *

other; while the interior is a jumbled composition of arabesque and gilding, windows of stained glass and wicker-work, and semicircular arches. At the upper end is an elaborately carved bronze pulpit, and portions of the floor are tesselated in mosaic.

I noticed that the worshipping-place of the men was covered with carpeting, while that of the women was spread with tattered matting! On leaving El-Aksa, we directed our steps to " Sedna Esa," the reputed cradle of our Saviour, but it was unfortunately closed. Such a number of women were around the Golden Gate during the whole time we were in the enclosure, that we did not dare to approach it, which I very much regretted. But a spot of still deeper interest was yet to be visited — the world-renowned Mosque of Omar : and we now directed our steps to one of its four entrances— an ornamental portal, its roof supported with slender Corinthian pillars. A " dim religious light" pervaded the building, and such a deep gloom the lofty dome, that it was scarcely possible to distinguish its rich gilding and arabesque. Just enough light penetrated the windows to produce an indescribably soft, and at the same time grand, effect.

It being an unusual thing for females (who, in Mohammedan estimation, are no better than brutes) to pollute with their presence so holy a place, we were closely questioned by the keeper, who luxuriated in a lazy attitude on the floor. The reply he received seemed perfectly to satisfy him, though unknown to me, being uttered in too low a tone to reach any but his own ear. He supplied us with a few tapers, and we descended by a flight of stone steps into the Cave of the Sakhrah, which it is supposed occupies the site of the Holy of Holies. Half way down the stairs is a colossal tongue, sculptured in alto relievo on the rock, which the "Faithful" devoutly kiss; and in the floor of the cave is a marble slab, which, on being struck, yields a hollow sound, indicative of a large void below. The traditions connected with these and other relics, such as the print of the Prophet's foot, I need not repeat, so very puerile are they. Over the Sakhrah hangs a time-worn red and green satin canopy, the gift of the Sultan.

It was not deemed safe to linger here more than a quarter of an hour, as the mosque was rapidly filling with the devout and faithful; yet it was with no little regret that I allowed myself so short a time on the hallowed ground, which I felt sure was once covered by the glorious Temple. Impressed with this belief, I imagined that every precious stone, imbedded within these walls, might once have composed part of the sacred structure.

Near the doorway through which we made our exit is a beautiful lilliputian building—a miniature of the mosque—marking the spot said to have been occupied by Solomon, when overseeing the erection of the Temple. Frolicking upon its marble floor were scores of laugh·

ing children. Scattered around are many light
and fantastic templets, but none so beautiful as
that appropriated by these children as their
playhouse. What a contrast between this fairy
scene and the dark filthy archways through
which we now groped our way on returning
home!

On reaching my own door, what was my
surprise on being saluted and welcomed in
Arabic—so completely metamorphosed was I
by my Turkish dress! I was greatly amused,
and determined to enjoy the joke, and retain
my incognito as long as possible. Accordingly, I remained perfectly silent, and kept
every feature in strict abeyance. Coffee was
handed, which I sipped with gravity quite as
apropos as the Oriental posture I had taken
on the divan : and in this position I sat many
minutes before I was recognised by the occupants of my own home, whose astonishment
was very great on hearing the English language
from such an unexpected source!

CHAPTER XI.

VISIT TO THE TOMB OF DAVID.

EARLY one morning, during the feast of Rhamadan, I was called to the parley room to see one of my friends, who rejoices in the name of the great Lawgiver of Israel. This liberalized little sprig of nobility having become rather a frequent visiter, I was at first inclined to excuse myself; but remembering he had lately hinted at the possibility of my gaining an entrance into the Tomb of David, I immediately obeyed the summons, and was soon convinced by his mysterious manner, that my pleasing anticipations were not unfounded. The door was closed and the most profound secrecy enjoined. Then laying his ponderous turban on the divan beside him, doffing his slippers, and crossing his legs, he proceeded to disclose the nature of his errand. In short, I was informed that his amiable and affectionate sister was ready for an adventure, and being in the same mood, we were not long in reaching Turfendah's home, where we found her busily engaged in selecting clothes, suitable for my disguise. A maid was summoned, at whose mercy I was placed, and she forthwith proceeded to dress me in a robe and trousers of the finest Damascus silk, a girdle of cashmere, and tunic of light blue, embroidered in silver flowers. My hands were already dyed with henna, having undergone this process on the occasion of a similar adventure in the Mosque of Omar, and they still retained the deep orange hue, without which my disguise would have been incomplete. My face too was pretty deeply tanned from a residence of several years, under a burning Syrian sun, which was quite an addition to my Turkish appearance. The sheet, veil, and slippers, came in due order, and having secreted my pencil and sketch-book, we sallied forth, accompanied by Turfen-dah's favorite slave.

The reputed Tomb of David is just outside the Zion Gate, hard by the Cœnaculum. It is surrounded by an irregular pile of buildings, and surmounted by a dome and minaret. In the interior are some of the most grotesque architectural embellishments imaginable, on the capitals of its ancient pillars—the remains of the times of the crusaders. Just think—the frightful owl occupying the place of the classic acanthus and the mythic lotus! We passed through several halls and corridors, evidently of the style of the Quixotic era of the crusaders' domination, before reaching the consecrated apartment, whose entrance is guarded by double iron doors. An old Derwish was pros-trate before the door on the cold stone floor. Not being privileged as ourselves to enter the sacred precincts, he was content with gazing at the tomb through the iron bars, for it is a rare thing that even a Mussulman ecclesiastic can gain admittance—my companion and her family enjoying this privilege only on account of their near relationship to the curator of the tomb. Our slave was despatched for the key, which she had no difficulty in obtaining, on the plea that her mistress wished to pray on the holy spot. But what was my consternation on seeing another slave return with her! I confess that I trembled, and was thinking I had better leave my awkward slippers behind in case of retreat, as they would greatly impede my progress, and thereby cause me to lose my head! But, after peering under my veil, and asking who I was, she seemed satisfied with the careless reply of Turfendah, that I was a friend of hers from Stamboul, and then invited us up stairs to see the keeper's hareem. The invitation was very graciously received by Dahudeiah, the wife of the young Effendi; who is always glad to vary the purgatory of a life with her husband by a visit to this place; for I can

16

testify, from personal observation, that the young Effendi lords it over her in true Oriental style. But Turfendah, thinking it more politic to decline, regretted "she was unfit to make a visit just at that time, feeling much exhausted from fasting." To our great relief the slave now left, and having dismissed the Derwish, the doors were closed and doubly locked.

The room is small in dimensions, but gorgeously furnished by the Sultan, I am told, who renews the tapestry every few years. The tomb is an immense sarcophagus of stone, covered with greenish satin tapestry embroidered with gold. To this a piece of black velvet is attached, with inscriptions from the Koran. A satin canopy of red, green, blue, and yellow stripes, hangs over the tomb, and tapestry of velvet richly embroidered in silver covers a door in one end of the room, leading to a cave immediately underneath. Silver candlesticks and golden vessels containing rose water, stand in different parts of the room, and a lamp hangs in the window, which is kept constantly burning, and whose wick, though saturated with oil, and I dare say a most nauseous dose, my companion eagerly swallowed, muttering a prayer with the usual attitudes of deep humility. After prostrating herself many times, she raised the covering of the tomb and rapturously kissed it. The ceiling is vaulted, the walls covered with blue porcelain in floral figures, while the floor is of highly polished marble of various colors. Having remained here an hour or more, and completed my sketch, we left in high glee at our success; but much greater was my rejoicing when I found myself at home—once more out of danger and out of my awkward costume.

CHAPTER XII.

TURKISH WEDDING.

The expected wedding of the lordly little Effendi Moosa and the gentle Dahudeiah, had been the topic of conversation for some time in Jerusalem, and a very brilliant "Fantazea" was anticipated by all the Turkish gossips, who discussed the matter between their sips of coffee and puffs at the chibouque. Mother and myself were fortunate enough to be among the invited guests; and on the appointed day a slave was sent to accompany us to the house of the Bash Catib, where the entertainment was to take place. The male portion, as a matter of course, was excluded from all insight into the tabooed cloisters of these secluded beings. After threading a few dark archways, the

(184)

servant halted at rather a loftier door than is usually seen in Oriental dwellings, and we were met by half a dozen slaves, who conducted us up several flights of gloomy steps, and through as many walled courts, into a spacious apartment where a real Arabian-night-entertainment scene presented itself. On the divan, which extended all around the room, were gracefully lolling about a hundred Turkish ladies of the élite of Jerusalem, each one sipping an exquisite little fingân of coffee, or smoking a chibouque gilded and mounted with an amber mouth-piece.

Several dancing-women were moving in undulating (and but for their trailing robes and trousers), even graceful steps, rattling little bells placed on the forefinger and thumb of each hand as they danced; while two or three more sat on a rug playing the tambourine and thrumming a red morocco drum-like instrument, producing anything but music. On our entrance each one saluted us in the

16 *

graceful style of the East, and some lovely little children ran to kiss our hands. The only daughter of the Bash Catib was present, and as usual received the homage paid her on all occasions, from the fact of her meritorious pilgrimage to Mecca. Her dress I noticed as extremely chaste and simple, in contrast with the gorgeous costumes and profusion of ornaments worn by the others. It consisted merely of white merino trousers and tunic spangled with small specks of gold, a light gauze turban, and the usual yellow slippers—her hands wanting the almost indispensable henna with which those of the rest were dyed in curious and fantastic figures. We were not long seated before the everlasting fingân of piping hot coffee was served, which we swallowed down philosophically, notwithstanding we knew from sad experience that a burnt tongue would be the inevitable consequence. The loud peal of the muezzim was soon heard calling the "faithful" to prayers, and several of the elderly ladies,

more devout than the rest, after washing their
hands and feet, immediately commenced the
routine of the various postures of the Mohammedan prayers—the dancing, singing, tambourine music, and clapping of hands, going on
during the whole time. Prayers being over, a
stool inlaid with pearl was set before us, on
which was placed a large round copper tray,
filled with a great variety of little salmagundi
dishes. Many of these diminutive tables were
spread, and cushions were laid around them
for the accommodation of the guests. A nap-
kin fringed with gold was handed to each, and
we, being Franks, were allowed the luxury of
coarse wooden spoons. The others, *sans* knives,
sans forks, *sans* spoons, as a matter of course
ate with their hands; and it was curious, to
say the least of it, to see their jewelled and
henna-dyed fingers dipping into a greasy dish
of rice, and cramming their mouths to an extent almost incredible! The dishes, notwithstanding their excessive richness, were quite

palatable; one, of the consistency of paste, composed of gum arabic, sugar, and a variety of nuts, was extremely pleasant.

Late in the afternoon I noticed each one equipping herself in her sheet and boots, and on inquiring the reason of such a bustle, found they were all going in procession to Neby Daûd, the residence of the bride, to conduct her from thence by torch-light to the dwelling of her future husband. Readily consenting to accompany them, I soon found myself in the midst of a long string of ghostly white sheets, winding through the innumerable dark alleys of the Jewish quarter. The Pilgrim led the train, and, being in delicate health, rode a horse splendidly caparisoned. On reaching Neby Daûd, we were shown into a large upper apartment, where the bride sat on a raised throne as immovable as a statue, and completely enveloped in a large red sheet. An altar adorned with silver censers fuming with incense, and tall candlesticks ornamented with gilt leaves, stood in front of her, while a sheathed sword hung over her head.

, Having partaken of coffee and sherbet, we were sprinkled with rose water and perfumed with incense. A company of hired women in the mean time kept up a constant clapping of hands and shrill singing, or rather screaming, about the "arroos" and "arreess" (bride and groom), until dark, when, fortunately for my aching head, they ceased at the approach of thirty or forty of their lords, who had come from the city. In the midst of this train the bridegroom walked under a canopy accompanied by torch-bearers and a fantastically dressed clown. On their arrival, the little groom was led up stairs to the bride, whose veil he raised to obtain a first glimpse of her face—then suddenly extinguished the only lighted candle, afterwards making a mock attempt to relight it. In total darkness the whole company, bride, groom, and all, rushed down stairs. The little pair were placed under a canopy; the torches were lighted, and amid the shrill screaming of the women, the beating of the tambourine and "tom-tom," accompanied by the blowing of a loud whistle, the procession again moved on. The torch-bearers led the train, then a long string of turbans, and in their midst the canopy held aloft by four bearers, while the white-sheeted throng followed behind.

On arriving at the Bash Catib's house, the bride and groom were conducted into separate apartments, where each was gorgeously attired: the bride in a perfect blaze of jewels and cloth of gold, wearing a gilded mitre on her head, ornamented with diamond stars and crescents. Her hands, face and feet, which before had been dyed with henna, were covered with pieces of gold foil, cut in odd shapes and figures; and her eyebrows and eyelids were stained black with khol. Beneath a hazy veil of gauze, spangled with gold, she tottered to a raised throne. After seating herself, several attendints gathered around and arranged not only the folds of her robe, but her very eyelids, which she carefully closed, accompanied by a caution not to open them. Her hands were then placed on her knees, and a slave stationed at her back, holding in her hand a drawn sword.

A little wax-doll-like creature, sitting perfectly motionless, and rigged up as she was, the figure on the throne now looked as much unlike a human being as can well be conceived. This little couple were mere children : the bride being nine and the groom twelve years of age ! Not uncommon ages, however, for the perpetration of matrimony in this country.

The entrance of the groom was now hailed by loud shouts from the women, and he also was placed on a throne at the upper end of the court in which we were assembled, beneath an immense tent, erected entirely over the court for this especial occasion. Seeing a smoking substance on a stand before the throne,

I drew near to ascertain from what it proceeded. Finding nothing but burning crusts of bread, I was puzzled to know the meaning of such a singular ceremony; but received no explanation, except that it was quite an indispensable form. Retreating to my first place of observation, I amused myself by watching the scene immediately before the throne. Two dancing-women danced in rapid motions, and each held tall wax candles in her hands, which threw their flitting shadows in every direction over the assembly.

The bride was now conducted to the middle of the court, two attendants supporting her train, and a slave bearing the sword before her. Slowly she came bowing her head from side to side, and holding her hands before her face. Here the groom met her, again drew aside her veil, and the august little pair were together led to one of the thrones — glad, no doubt, to rest awhile from the fatiguing ordeal. The Pilgrim made way through the crowd with a seat, and placed it directly in front of the little couple for me to sketch them—exclaiming to the people to make way for the "bint-el-Hakim"—daughter of the doctor.

During all these quaint and unmeaning ceremonies, the women continued clapping their hands, beating the tambourine, and singing loudly in eulogy of the bride and groom, whose noisy nuptials we now had the extreme satisfaction of hearing were completed. Suffice it to say, that with a headache, and a terrific roaring in the ears, we returned home about nine o'clock at night, notwithstanding the earnest entreaties of the ladies to remain all night, and partake of two or three more suppers.

At a Jewish wedding I afterwards attended, the ceremonies were somewhat similar to these, but even more unmeaning and complex. The little Jewish couple—the groom about thirteen years of age and the bride eleven—sat under a canopy of brocaded gold much more lofty and

17

splendid than that of the Turkish pair; and in lieu of extinguishing a light, a goblet of wine was dashed to pieces at their feet. The ceremonies of these Oriental weddings, though sadly altered, still remind one very much of those mentioned in the Bible.

CHAPTER XIII.

SHOPPING EXPEDITON.

THE bazaars of no Oriental city are comparable to those of Damascus, a city which is so beautiful in every respect, that Mohammed dared not look upon it, fearing that he should find so entrancing an earthly paradise as entirely to rob him of any desire to reach that of the skies. But Damascus is not Jerusalem, and as everybody likes to know how one goes shopping in Jerusalem, I shall not withhold a description of its bazaars because of their small share of attractiveness. True, the idea of shopping in Jerusalem is not a very poetical one, and some, I dare say, suppose it is an unpractised art in this city of hallowed associations. But not so think the residents, who, notwithstanding the

indifference of the shops, find an occasional
visit to them quite an indispensable requisite
to their comfort. My first expedition of this
kind, apart from the novelty, afforded me but
little satisfaction. Being uninitiated, I gladly
accepted the offer of several of my Turkish
friends to accompany me, who called quite
early in the morning, that we might devote
several hours to this all-absorbing feminine
occupation, and the remainder of the day to a
bath. Many quiet streets were threaded before
joining the busy crowd which thronged the
bazaars.

Jerusalem being a spot of so much attraction
to every nation under heaven, we here see
every variety of costume, making the bazaars
a continual carnival. One moment you are
greeted with a garb betokening the highest civil-
ization, and the next, with the coarse camel's
hair garment of a Bedawin from the burning
sands of the desert. At one step you meet the
black silk wrappings of the Egyptian women,

and the next, the ghostly white robes of her Syrian sister. But nothing can compare, in richness and beauty, with the flowing robes and full white turban of her lord and master. The wayfaring man wears a girdle which is so arranged that one end answers the purpose of a bag, in which he carries his money, valuables, and other small articles; and in his bosom may be found his balances, which every Oriental carries at all times, with which the coin is weighed and by which its value is determined—and if accompanied by his wife and children, you will be reminded of the words of Isaiah: "They shall bring their sons in their arms, and their daughters shall be carried on their shoulders." The woman occasionally carries her child on her shoulders, with a water-skin on her back.

Along the dark and narrow alleys rather than streets we groped our way, now retreating within a door at the approach of the towering camel, and now hastily stepping out of the way of a string of donkeys trudging along under

17 *

a load of brush of gigantic dimensions. This is intended for fuel, and reminds one of the expression used by our Saviour: "The grass which to-day is, and to-morrow is cast into the oven," a passage which greatly perplexes those living in a country whose wide-spread forests afford abundance of material for fuel. But in the Holy Land, which is so scantily supplied with trees, the passage is perfectly applicable, for in the absence of wood, necessity compels the people to burn brush, roots, dried grasses, and weeds of all kinds, so plentifully growing in the fields; and immense donkey-loads are daily brought to the city for this purpose. Thorns also, which grow in great profusion, are used as fuel, and explain the figures used in Ecclesiastes: "As the crackling of thorns under a pot, so is the laughter of a fool;" and in Isaiah, "As thorns cut up they shall be burned in the fire."

There is a ditch in the centre of most of the streets, but there are no sidewalks and no pavements, for the unevenly laid stones do not deserve the name; nor are there any lamp-posts. At night you see here and there the dim flickering of a little earthen lamp of olive oil beside a reclining figure of a man, who lies sleeping upon a raised platform in front of his bazaar; and this is the only light one enjoys in a nocturnal walk through the city. Hence the necessity of carrying our own lamp—a necessity which is still farther enforced by the regulation inflicting fine and imprisonment upon all who are caught in the street without a light after an early hour. The streets are lined with bare stone walls of prison-like houses, broken by a very few, and very small, latticed windows, and covered usually with arches, or pieces of matting, stretched from house to house—the walls generally ruined, and the matting always tattered. Thus, Jerusalem wears an air of gloom and misery, and its inhabitants move about in keeping with the wretchedness of the streets and houses. It is impossible to discern

a glad face among them, and the camels carefully plant their feet, noiselessly pursuing their
way as if intuitively afraid of breaking the
silent gloom.   Suddenly, however, we enter a
street where the people move more briskly—
the camels are hurried along by loud threats
from their drivers, and the shopmen still more
loudly proclaim the merits of their wares.
Country women are seated on the sides of the
streets with baskets of fruits and vegetables.
The shops of the dry goods venders are nothing more than rows of small platforms, four
or five feet square, with shelves arranged
around them on which the goods are placed.
The purchaser stands in the street, while the
merchant indolently reclines on a rug spread
over the platform.   With utter indifference he
lays aside his narghileh, and at first seems very
careless whether we buy or not; but presently
launches into great volubility on the excellence of his fabrics. Oriental bazaars have not
the least pretensions to taste, but often make

a great display of richly embroidered goods. A white handkerchief is unfolded, which, although embroidered in gold, is of the coarsest cotton, and tears in the opening. Speaking of taste, reminds me that, among other purchases of one of my companions, was a spool of white cotton, with which she intended making up her robe of black silk!

Huge piles of slippers are tumbled from the shelves—some of the plain yellow morocco, without ornament, and others with embroidery and rosettes of pearls enclosing colored stones—embroidered jackets of purple—cotton velvet worked with tinsel and bright silks, or gold and silk braid—caps of scarlet cloth with high raised gold work, and tassels half a yard in length—striped silk sashes from Damascus—napkins perfumed with otto of rose, and embroidered in the corners—ready made trowsers, and red fez caps without seam. Calicoes are not only rare, but almost worthless, and their prices nearly as high as those of silks. Further on is a fancy shop, with sparkling cut glass narghilehs, and little coffee-cup stands of richly embossed silver —Mohammed's prohibition of silver to the contrary notwithstanding. For these they charge a hundred piastres, or five dollars. Other trinkets of hareem use are here displayed, and next is the drug bazaar, where all kinds of spices, drugs and perfumes, are sold. Otto of roses, as well as rose water, made from the roses of Wady el Werd (valley of roses), can be bought at a marvelously low price. Further on, the respectable Armenian is seen manufacturing small trinkets and trifles with his scanty supply of instruments; and those, of the rudest manufacture. With them, however, he forms a ring, or sets an amulet, with wonderful skill. Interspersed among these are shops where bushels of beads are displayed, made of camel's bone, amber, sandal, and olive wood; then there are amulets, blood stones from India, and trinkets in pearl, made, by the Bethlehemites, in imitation of the Church of the Holy Sepulchre, and a

long catalogue of saints which are in great
requisition among the devout pilgrims. Here
and there a man may be seen standing by a
small earthen furnace of embers, across which
he throws wires strung with small pieces of
mutton—a very popular dish. The bazaar is
densely crowded with shrouded women and
pilgrims from all parts of the world, and the
air resounds with the screams of the camel
and donkey drivers. Rooh, dahrac, woojac,
they cry—"stand aside, your back, your face,"
which, united to the babel of languages, and
the fierce gesticulation, characteristic of Orientals, presents a scene of noise and confusion
completely bewildering. Add to this the braying of donkeys, the growling of camels, the clattering of horses' hoofs on the uneven stones,
one's care to avoid, at every step, the accumulated heaps of filth and debris, and the hot
rays of the sun piercing through the ragged
matting overhead, and the reader may be content with the picture without wishing to participate in the reality.

CHAPTER XIV.

HAVING escaped the noisy bazaar, I was invited by my kind companions, Turfendah and her friends, to take dinner with them, and afterwards repair to the bath. Oriental women frequently spend the entire day at the bath; but from what I had heard and read of the ordeal, I congratulated myself that such was not the present plan.

On knocking at the gloomy gateway of their home, we were speedily admitted by the slaves; and on entering the house, found a very tempting dinner already laid out on several diminutive tables, arranged around the room. (For in this country you do not go to the table; but the table is brought to you.)

Having concluded our repast of all manner of curious little dishes, preparations were commenced for the very important occupation of the afternoon. Baskets were loaded with oranges, lemons, coffee, coffee-pots, fingâns, pipes, all the ingredients necessary for making sherbet, hand mirrors, fresh, fair linen in quantities, and perfumery. With these on their arms, the slaves followed us to one of the finest bathing establishments in the city. Having paid the usual bucksheesh at the door of six piastres, or thirty cents, I was conducted into a large domed room where numbers of women and children were engaged in robing themselves for departure, having spent all the morning in the intricate processes yet in reservation for us. The temperature here was very cool; the light was admitted through the dome, and rugs were laid in the alcoves around the room for our accommodation.

Suspended on strings stretched from wall to wall, quantities of linen were placed for the

18

use of the bathers, while passing through the
different halls, making quite useless our precaution of bringing a supply. The baskets
being emptied, the narghilehs were filled with
water from the fountain in the middle of the
room, and a small bronze furnace of coals
brought in, over which the coffee soon sim-
mered in unison with the playing of the water;
and as the art of making coffee is a matter of
the highest importance in the East, and entirely unlike our mode of preparation, it should
not be passed over in silence.

The grains, having been slightly roasted, are
pounded in a mortar; adding a small quantity
of water, a vessel is filled which is kept constantly simmering by the fire, in order that it
may be ready for visiters at all hours of the
day. The number of guests having been
ascertained, the servant who has especial charge
of this department of domestic affairs, selects
a boiler of suitable size, in which he puts a
proper proportion of pounded coffee. He adds

to this, not pure water, but the liquid coffee, heated nearly to the boiling point. Having remained a moment over the fire, it is placed in small gilded and enamelled cups, with brazen, or even silver holders, like our own egg-cups. These holders are sometimes very costly, being made of gold, and set with precious stones, despite the canon of the Koran. The beverage is now ready for use, sugar and cream not being thought of, nor the process of clarifying; for the *grounds* or dregs are eagerly swallowed, and considered quite indispensable. In this way the aroma is preserved, which we only partially retain by our double refining process. The servant hands only one cup at a time, and, on presenting it, places his hand on his breast, and makes a profound salaam.

While the slave removes the pins from Turfendah's turban, she alternately sips her coffee, smokes her chibouque, and glances with surprise at the expertness of the Frank lady in unlinking hooks and eyes, which to her are the most mysterious things imaginable. The last sip of coffee taken, we were wrapped in sheets, and supplied with clogs, on which we clattered over the wet marble floor to the next hall. Here the temperature was warmer than that we had just left, but not uncomfortably so; and the water that was dashed on me being also pleasantly heated, the fears with which I had been inspired by accounts of the dreaded ordeal began to vanish; and I entertained the most friendly feelings towards the marble bathing tub, with the water gently flowing over me from an aperture in the wall. We passed through a third hall of an increased warmth of temperature into a fourth, which was filled with a dense vapor of suffocating heat.

Never did I long so intensely for a breath of fresh air, to which I resolved ever after to give due appreciation. In a little while, however, by dint of inward Medo-Persian resolves, I was enabled to brave my fate with better

nerve, and even to enjoy the ludicrous scene
around me. A dozen attendants were engaged
in pouring hot water on the crouching figures
of women and girls of every age. And now I
trembled as I saw one of the dreaded spectres
approach me with a vessel holding a gallon of
smoking hot water, with which, before I could
make the least remonstrance, I was completely
deluged.

An observant tourist has given this process
the very appropriate name of parboiling; and
up to the moment of actual trial, I had imagined it to be an exaggeration; but while re-
alizing the terrors of the word myself, from
sheer justice I withdrew the accusation. In
vain was I urged to consent to a repetition of
the operation. Finding me to be an unyield-
ing subject, my torturer covered me from head
to foot with soap-suds, and put in full operation
her horse-hair glove; and surely she imagined
herself scrubbing the floor, rather than a human being; or perhaps she had been an em-

18 *

ployee in the inquisition, and there learned to
practise this unmerciful treatment with such
consummate art. The second time I trem-
blingly beheld the approach of my torturer
with a vessel of water; but this time I franti-
cally dipped my finger in the water, and finding its temperature to be a decided improve-
ment on the first, I yielded a reluctant consent.
Bundles of the fibre of the palm were next
brought into requisition, which, being soft, and
gently applied, was a most agreeable substitute
for the coarse glove of camel's hair. Those
around me were now submitting to the joint-
cracking, limb-stretching, body-breaking processes; but I assured them I was perfectly
content with the skill already displayed, and
the pain already endured, and resisted every
entreaty with resolute firmness. I gladly remained a silent observer; and, on its conclu-
sion, joyfully resumed my sheet, and followed
the spectral train to the hall we had converted
into a dressing-room, where sherbet, coffee,

pipes, and goblets of the most delicious lemonade awaited us. Some were regaling themselves with olives, pistachio nuts, and watermelon seeds. Of the latter article they are very fond; and during the season of watermelons they carefully gather the seed, and dry and salt them for future use.

During the bath, slaves had busied themselves in making preparations for dyeing the hands of their mistresses with henna. A vessel of melted wax, rosin, and other ingredients unknown to me, was at hand, with which, by means of a steel wire resembling a knitting-needle, the slave traced the outlines of flowers and all kinds of curious figures on the outstretched hand of her mistress. The spaces between the figures were then filled up with this softened mixture, and, after allowing it to cool and become hardened, a large lump of henna made into dough was pasted over her hand, and the whole bound up, mummy-like, with several thicknesses of linen. The poor creature must allow her hands to remain in this helpless state a day and night; but no doubt feels amply rewarded for her pains on beholding the delicate orange-brown tracery on removing the dough, wax, and bandages. The feet are dyed in the same manner; and in summer, great pride is felt in the display of these unique slippers. The skin seldom retains the dye more than a month; but so indispensable a requisite to beauty is it esteemed by an Oriental woman, that she no sooner perceives the fading of this important addition to her charms, than the process is repeated; and she is thus never without this ingenious substitute for gloves—an article of attire they had never seen until their acquaintance with me—and great was their delight when I one day presented them with several pairs I had fashioned out of a piece of black lace.

As may be imagined, the whole afternoon

had now passed; and very serious thoughts were entertained, and soon put into execution, of taking our departure; and indeed the shades of night were already gathering around us before we reached our homes.

CHAPTER XV.

PEEP INTO A TURKISH HAREEM.

IT was with no little pleasure that I accepted
an invitation from the family of the Bash Catib,
whose office is next in rank to that of the
Pacha, to spend a day with them. They had
proved themselves true friends; but, apart from
this, I had long been anxious to obtain an insight into hareem life.

On entering the house I was greeted with
the usual cry of welcome, " Ahlan Wassahlan,"
in which every occupant of the hareem united.
Even the slaves ran to the door clapping their
hands and making the noisiest demonstrations
of delight. Five minutes after I had taken my
seat, fingâns of coffee and pipes were handed,
in which I attempted to join them, but the

(214)

effort proved a signal failure. The delicate workmanship of the tiny cups containing the coffee, by no means exempts one from a burnt tongue, nor makes palatable the unsweetened beverage—for the charm of Turkish coffee (with some!) consists in its being boiling hot, and the absence of sugar. The narghileh, so tempting to the eye, with its crystal urn and amber mouth-piece, was soon laid aside with a disgust which I fear was hardly understood by my Turkish friends, who so highly appreciate these luxuries that most of their time is devoted to their enjoyment.

There is but one Turkish lady on my list of acquaintances who can boast of her ability to read and write! Her presence afforded some variety to the trivial subjects generally discussed; for she not only possesses the rare accomplishments of reading and writing, but has improved them; and her conversation showed that she was conversant with the Koran and other text-books of Mohammedan faith. In addition to this, a pilgrimage to Mecca, and a hand ever ready to relieve the wants of the poor, have secured for her a wide-spread fame.

About noon, dinner was announced; not, however, before each one had washed her hands and face, and observed the usual forms of prayer. A large round waiter was placed on a stool richly inlaid with pearl, and upon it little dishes in endless variety were temptingly displayed. Among them, confections prepared from rose leaves and apricots, transparent jellies and soups composed of a variety of nuts. Cucumbers scooped out and filled with rice and minced meat, were a favorite dish; and another, almost as popular, was a bowl of minute cylinders of dough, dried in the sun, and then mixed in a sauce of butter and sugar. Cushions laid on the floor were substituted for chairs; but alas for knives and forks! In their stead my only resort was a wooden spoon. The favorite wife, and the Queen of the Hareem, frequently handed me morsels of food with her own henna-tipped fingers, intended as a mark of great honor.

Having done full justice to our elegant little dinner, the luxurious divan was resumed, and a warm discussion entered upon as to the manner of spending the afternoon. The bath was proposed by some, but a dissenting voice was heard from the seat of honor, where the chief lady gracefully reclined, in favor of music and dancing. A messenger was accordingly despatched for tambourines and dancing-women —for in the East dancing is considered far beneath any but the poorer class, who make it a trade, and charge a certain sum for their services on festive occasions. Their dancing consists in a few undulating movements of the body, not ungraceful, and accompanied by castanets and the tambourine.

My European dress caused them as much amusement as their curious apparel afforded me, and they were not satisfied until we had exchanged costumes. A mirror was brought

19

into requisition, in which they wonderingly surveyed the change wrought by the sport. A large number had assembled to see the lady from the "new world," and they were very curious to know something about the manners and customs of my country. Great was their surprise on hearing of the liberty enjoyed by their Western sisters, which, strange to say, although I used all the terms of enthusiasm my knowledge of Arabic could command, they did not seem at all to covet. They could not conceive of a woman possessing a soul. On asking one of them what would become of her after death, she replied, "I shall be put under the ground—nothing more." "And your husband," said I, "will he be doomed to the same fate?" "Oh, no," she sadly replied, "he will be taken above, and there enjoy all the delights of paradise."

Among them were some lovely Georgians, profusely adorned with sparkling jewels and the purest of Orient pearls; there were few

TURKISH DANCING GIRL AND HAREEM.

beside these with any pretensions to beauty. Nearly all, however, had the soft gazelle eye so often apostrophized by the poet.

I left them, feeling more grateful than ever for the light I enjoy, and the hope of a blissful immortality, and ardently desiring to share with them my own glorious civil and religious privileges, which would at once release them from the leading cause of their degradation— the tyranny exercised over them by their husbands, who can put them away for any reason, every reason, and no assignable reason.

I can but feel emotions of deepest indignation at the painful recollection of quite a pretty young girl, who was inhumanly divorced by her hard-hearted husband, before either of them was twelve years of age—simply because he saw a more beautiful girl, and was unfortunately able to buy her.   Oh! the inexpressible, and, by us, inconceivable wretchedness flowing from this awful traffic in female flesh—the burning shame and crying sin of Oriental life! Love, of course, is a plant that will thrive in no such soil. Indeed, it seems to be rather an exotic in the Orient at this day, cultivated only here and there as a mere hot-house plant.

While memory performs her functions, I shall never forget the impression made on my mind, when witnessing the anguish of a poor girl, as she went along weeping to the house of a brutal old one-eyed monster, who had bought her for his pandemonian hareem. Nor is it the father and husband alone that thus tyrannize over the degraded women of the East. The authority of the brother, in the event of the death of the father, even though the mother is still living, is quite as absolute. He can beat them without mercy and with impunity, and though he may be younger than his seven sisters, it is he alone that sells them to their heartless husbands, or in other words, to the master who will give most for them.

Happily now, however, this is rather a rare case, owing to the ascendancy of Frank influ-

ence.   Indeed, the Orientals are extremely im-
pressible by the example of their more civilized neighbors.   Several incidents may serve
to illustrate this.   On first arriving in Jerusalem, the male portion of the family were
always served first, when we were handed
refreshments at their houses; but, seeing that
we observed the very reverse order of things,
they soon imitated our example.   The veil has
also often been stealthily drawn aside, in imitation of our non-observance of this strange custom of smothering oneself.   In cases of cruel
treatment by their husbands, such as dashing
any missile at them which may chance to lie
in their way, beating them with sticks, and
otherwise causing the blood to flow, our remon-
strances have not unfrequently proved effectual.
As may be imagined, the more sensitive of these
maltreated creatures are thus rendered very
miserable, even entreating for poison in some
instances to put an end to their existence, as
well as that of their cruel masters.   It is well

19 *

known, that while Oriental women are taught
to believe that they have no souls, they are
impressed with the idea that their husbands
will revel in delight in the bowers of paradise,
where each will have a hareem of any number
of black-eyed houris, varying from seventy to
seventy thousand, to administer to his happiness. But, notwithstanding this, these de-
praved creatures are very religious, as far as
bodily exercise goes, strictly observing their
many fasts and festivals, and devoting much
of their time to prayer. And their prayers,
although so complicated, lengthy, and fatiguing,
are not confined to their mosques or their
homes, but, whether visiting or on any excursion of pleasure, they no sooner hear the sono-
rous voice of the muezzim, than their girdles,
sheets, or mats, are spread, their faces, arms,
hands, and feet bared, and they commence the
intricate process of prayer. Not twice or thrice
a day, but five times do these deluded creatures go through their genuflexions and pros-

trations; thus setting us an example, which, if imitated to but a limited extent, would prove a blessing not only to ourselves, but reflexly to them.

One day we had a visit from several of the hareems of the nobility, numbering twenty ladies and half as many slaves, and, although away from home, they sent their slaves to the well for water, performed their ablutions, and each one, immediately on the cry of the muezzim, devoutly prayed. Of course, their veils and sheets were laid aside, and I was not a little amused at the great commotion made by the sudden entrance into the court of a Turk, while they were eating with uncovered faces. The slaves set up a loud scream, and, terror-struck, ran in every direction for their mistress's veils. As for the mistresses themselves, it was actually distressing to hear their piercing cries —and such was their effect on the unfortunate intruder, that he made a precipitate retreat, amid shouts of "Roohee! roohee!"—away! away!

Gratitude is one of their redeeming qualities. What will the ungrateful lady of the Occident think of her Oriental sisters abasing themselves to kiss the feet of a dispenser of medicines, to show their appreciation of some slight medical services he may have rendered them? I have seen a lady of the upper circle of Jerusalem society struggling to perform this humiliating act, and this, too, in spite of an uncultivated mind and soul. The education of Oriental women is not only entirely neglected, but strongly reprobated by public sentiment—almost the sole arbiter of manners and customs in that country, if not in this. Indeed, must not this necessarily result from the contempt and servitude in which she is held? Among rich and poor, in the family of the Effendi and the Fellah, she is alike ignorant. Her accomplishments consist in being able to cook, arrange her turban tastefully, and administer to the every whim of her *doting* husband! Odious as he must too often be, yet she has no other God than her husband, and to gratify him with the strictest obedience is the most praiseworthy of all good works she can perform.

Has not the reader already concluded that there is but one Sun that can penetrate the darkness that envelopes these unhappy creatures—the Sun of Righteousness! It delivers her from her present oppression and future punishment. How important, then, to light up in her mind the knowledge that she possesses an immortal soul! How binding upon us to inspire her with the hope of heaven! How urgent the call upon our sympathy and benevolence! How plaintively the cry comes wailing across the waters, not from the man of Macedonia, but from the poor degraded woman of the land of Sarah and the Marys—" Come over and help us !"

CHAPTER XVI.

DOMESTIC ARCHITECTURE.

IN order to convey an idea of the domestic architecture of Jerusalem, it may be well to give a description of one of the private houses, which will serve as a specimen of the whole. I will therefore introduce the reader into our home, situated in the Jewish quarter, and occupying one of the most interesting localities in Jerusalem. An arched doorway leads into a large court paved with stones, and surrounded partly by a wall and partly by rooms. During the sickly season there may be seen crowds of sick persons impatiently waiting in this court to be admitted into the *hackmè* or dispensary, which, together with the stable, opens on one side of this square court, while opposite, is a

MEHHEMEH, OR TURKISH COUNCIL CHAMBER.

little elevated garden of oleanders, rosemary, and other shrubbery, surrounded by a stone wall. The kitchen, however, is the most important and unique feature of the court—it consists of a small room with abundance of tonjeras (Arab copper kettles) of all sizes, from a gallon to a pint, and a solitary frying-pan, brought from across the waters. The fireplace is altogether different from our ideas of a fire-place. Built against one side of the room is a projecting table of stone and plaster work in which rows of ovens are scooped out, with grates laid across them for burning charcoal. A staircase leads directly over this unique kitchen into a small upper court opening into a chamber and dining room. Passing through the latter, we find ourselves on the housetop, surrounded by a wall about five feet high; and how often have I walked on this terrace and plucked a drooping blade—bringing to mind the emblematical allusion of the sweet singer of Israel to its stunted growth and withered

appearance. Constantly exposed to a burning
sun, and having for its soil only the plaster
connecting the stones, its frailty affords the
Psalmist a fit emblem of the sudden destruction of those who despise the interests of
Zion—

> " They shall be ashamed and turned back,
>   All those that hate Zion.
>   They shall be as grass upon the housetops,
>   Which, before one plucks it, withers away,
>   With which the mower fills not his hand,
>   Nor the sheaf-binder his arms."

The flat roofs of Oriental houses afford a
most striking illustration of numberless Scriptural allusions, but imperfectly understood by
the occupant of houses with pointed roofs.
The Orientals spend much of their time on
the housetop, which is of easy access by
flights of stone steps, and they are generally
surrounded by a wall of sufficient height to
conceal their occupants from view even of
those on the roofs of adjoining houses. Hence

we cannot accuse Peter of giving publicity to his devotions when he resorted to the housetop to pray. Small chambers are sometimes built in the corner of the wall; and in these little kioscos the inmates of the house spend most of their time during summer, but they cannot be used during the inclement season; for, besides their exposed situation, they are lightly built for the sake of coolness during warm weather. But, notwithstanding, they are sometimes very damp and uncomfortable. Solomon says, "It is better to dwell in the corner of a housetop than in a wide house with a brawling woman."

In the middle of the floor is the mouth of one of the tanks or wells—recalling another Scriptural incident. It was in one of these wells or cisterns that the woman at Bahurim concealed Jonathan and Ahimaaz from the messengers sent by Absalom in pursuit of them. In different parts of the house are several wells opening into the courts, and I

20

often recall the narrative on seeing the floor
of the court covered with corn or wool spread
out to dry in the sun, for the well at Bahurim
was in a court, and its mouth was hid by
covering it with corn. These cisterns are
sometimes dry, and it was at such a time, of
course, that this ruse was resorted to.

We are now standing high above the valley
of the Tyropœon, and just opposite Mount
Olivet and the Temple enclosure. We are
a hundred feet above the huts in the valley called the Mugrabin quarter—the house
standing on a bold rock projecting from the
most precipitous part of Mount Zion. In its
rocky base are caves into which we at one
time contemplated a retreat for safety when
the city and surrounding country were first
convulsed by the Turco-Russian war.

I shall not soon forget the deep anxiety and
dread we all experienced soon after war was
declared, when the fanatical spirit of the Fellahin was first aroused. We had learned from

the proprietor of "the Tombs of the Kings,"
that a royal sarcophagus had been discovered
in one of its recesses, a few years previous, and
removed to the Mechemeh, or Congressional
Hall of Jerusalem, now identified as occupying
the site of the "Council Chamber," or Sanhe-
drim. Permission for a visit had been obtained
from the proper authorities, and I was sitting
there taking a sketch of the room and its contents, greatly enjoying myself, when the Bash
Catib's servant came running in, almost breathless, and with the deepest anxiety depicted in
his countenance (for he had all along shown
us much courtesy and kindness), told us
to flee for our lives — that the Fellahin had
taken the city! We accordingly fled to our
premises with all haste, and barricadoed the
doors as best we could. But before we could
make sure our defence, he came running, with
joy now lighting up his face, to inform us that
though they had entered the city in large num-

bers, they were not armed; and were being turned out as rapidly as possible.

This valley, which is no other than the Ty-ropœon or Cheesemongers' Valley of Josephus, was once spanned by the magnificent bridge so much admired by the Queen of Sheba on her memorable visit to its architect King Solomon. Its remains still exist, and astonish the travel-ler by the immense size of the arched stones. About thirty miles distant are the mountains of Moab, which, at certain parts of the day, vie with the skies in their rich and ever vary-ing tints. At our right, Mount Zion is covered with picturesque and dilapidated old buildings, standing boldly against a background of sky. A solitary palm tree, thick groves of cactus, and the notched battlements of the city walls, complete the landscape.

This site is reckoned one of the most notable in the city; for it was on this "stronghold of Zion" that all the rulers of Judea, from King Jebus down to King Agrippa, built their mag-

nificent palaces; and its present remains show
that it was either the site of a crusader's
church, or that of the palace of the Frank
king.

Retracing our steps, and descending a narrow stairway, we emerge into a court with a
circular skylight over the lower end, but
covered at the upper by an arched ceiling. A
tent is stretched over the skylight, and this
part of the court is converted into a chapel.
All around, are chambers with vaulted ceilings,
and windows guarded with iron bars.   The
exterior of the house has the appearance of an
old castle, or rather prison, for the windows are
not only few and small, but add still more to
its prison-like appearance by their massive iron
bars, an inseparable part of every house in the
East.   Suliman Effendi, however, a wealthy
Turkish resident of Jerusalem, has lately astonished his neighbors by furnishing his windows
with green Venetian blinds, giving his house
quite a modern appearance.

20 *

CHAPTER XVII.

THE MOHAMMEDANS.

"Jerusalem, Jerusalem,
Thy cross is on thee now!
An iron yoke is on thy neck,
And blood is on thy brow;
Thy golden crown, the crown of truth,
Thou didst reject as dross,
And now thy cross is on thee laid—
The Crescent is thy Cross!".

NOWHERE on the wide globe do we find religion manifested in so many forms, and to such a degree, as in Jerusalem. Not a pure and undefiled religion which consists in visiting the fatherless and widow, and living the holy and humble life pointed out and exhibited by our Divine Master, but that of which form, bigotry, and parade are the chief characteristics. Look at that haughty Turk, as he fingers his beads and treads the silent bazaar with a step so proud and stately, reminding one of the self-satisfied Pharisee in the parable! He thinks, forsooth, because he has just prostrated himself again and again on the marble floor of yon gorgeous mosque, in adoration of the false Prophet, that the gates of Paradise are already opened wide for his entrance. Yet this same son of delusion, shrinks not from the commission of every imaginable sin, each of which he esteems as nought, so long as he strictly observes the feasts, fasts, and ceremonies of his creed. He finds the lax principles of the Koran, and the pleasure of his pipe, unfailing panaceas for any qualms of conscience that may arise—if conscience he has; but of this one is constrained to believe that these benighted creatures are entirely bereft. Should he, in his dealings with a Jew, cheat him of his last para, spit upon and curse him, he imagines it is all quite proper, and even praiseworthy. He takes delight in buffeting him, and counts it his chiefest pleasure to do him all manner of harm. And not only so, but teaches his children and children's children to treat every son of Israel as they would the dogs that infest the streets, knowing full well that the downtrodden Jew cannot resist their bitter persecutions; for the Turks are the despots of the land, and to their iron rod the fallen race of Israel must submit. But should this devotee of Islamism fail to wash his hands before praying, or neglect to fall down and call upon the false prophet five times a day, he would consider himself guilty of grievous sins, so implicit is his reliance upon form alone. They have no bells, nor will they permit the Christians the general use of them. The cry of the muezzim, which calls them to prayers, is their substitute; and wherever they may chance to be, or whatever their engagements, they instantly obey the summons, and perform numberless kneelings, bowings, prostrations, and unmeaning gesticulations.

The greatest of their ceremonials is Rhamadan—a fast of twenty-nine days; but while all food is abstained from during the day, each night is spent in riotous feasting and carousing. Much parade is made, for they are determined their religion shall not be "hid under a bushel." Seven deafening salutes come booming twice a day from the battery on the heights of the Hippic tower, and the loud wailing cries of the muezzim are heard day and night from every minaret in the city. The feast of Biram, which immediately follows these observances, continues three days, and is considered by the people as a time of great rejoicing.

The Derwishes who are selected for the office of muezzim, are always chosen from the blind, if practicable. This precaution is taken in order to prevent them from seeing the women who may be walking unveiled in their gardens below, or seated on the house-tops.

Another prominent ceremonial is their yearly pilgrimage to the Tomb of Moses, which they pretend to have discovered on this side of Jordan, notwithstanding the declaration that his burial-place is on the other side, and "is not known to this day." The pilgrims form an immense cavalcade, and having with difficulty made their way through the narrow streets of Jerusalem, a halt is made outside St. Stephen's Gate, and a most cruel ceremony practised before the eyes of the admiring multitude. A splendid charger, with gay trappings, is brought forward, and mounted by some church or civil dignitary, who rides over the bodies of any of the "*Faithful*" who may possess the requisite zeal to prostrate themselves, and submit to the terrible ordeal; and many are so infatuated as joyfully to endure the test.

Methinks, with every reader of these incidents of error, superstition, and ignorance, the following question will arise :—If these poor creatures are so strict in the performance of these onerous rites, thereby risking even life itself, should not we, who are enlightened Christians, feel constrained to observe with tenfold greater zeal the just and righteous commands of the meek and lowly Jesus?

The Mohammedan citizens of Jerusalem reside on Bezetha in great numbers, and their Derwishes occupy cloisters within the enclosure of the Mosque of Omar. Their mosques are generally devoid of ornament, having only quotations from the Koran inscribed upon the walls and doors; but all are provided with cisterns for the performance of their ablutions, and a niche in the wall indicating the direction of Mecca, toward which they always turn their faces when engaged in prayer. During their services some of the Derwishes convert themselves into so many tops, incessantly whirling and spinning round and round, until one is expecting every moment to see them drop from dizziness.

With the Mohammedans, the shaving of the

head is never neglected; leaving only a small tuft of hair by which they believe Mohammed will elevate them bodily to heaven on the resurrection day.

Such is the absurdity of some of their practices, that a Turk thinks it a great sacrilege to sneeze without audibly thanking Heaven that Shatan (the devil) did not seize so excellent an opportunity of jumping down his throat.

They almost universally allow their beards to grow, and such is the importance attached to this appendage, that the common compliment of the day is, " May your beard attain a great length !"

Infidels and skeptics, in attacking Christianity, have endeavored to place Mohammedanism upon the same level, and attach to it the same importance. To succeed in this attempt, they must elevate a false religion to the standard of the holiest and purest faith the world has ever known. In so doing, their object is to degrade Christianity, and to place its author by the side of Mohammed as the founder of a sect.

The chief arguments of this class of opponents to the Christian religion, are based upon a supposed analogy between the character of Christ and Mohammed, their prominent doctrines, and the rapid dissemination of both throughout the most civilized nations of the earth ; which arguments, being a mixture of truth and error, and having found a lodgement in the unreflecting mind, are worthy of consideration.

A glance at the life of this self-styled " Prophet of God," may, *perhaps,* enable us to discover this boasted analogy :

Mohammed was born at Mecca A. D. 569. His family was one of the most honorable in Arabia : they were wealthy, learned, and occupied a high and influential position in the government of their country. Abu Taleb, his uncle, was the President of Mecca, and was High Priest to the idol of the Black Stone.

21

His caravans to Syria were sometimes accompanied by the young Arab, where he doubtless heard the Gospel of Christ proclaimed, and became familiar with its truths, for the reception of which his mind had been prepared by the story of Jesus, told him by his mother, who, though the wife of Abdallah, was a reputed Jewess.

At the age of twenty-five, Mohammed was said to be the handsomest man of the tribe Koreish; and soon after married the rich and noble widow Khadijah, thus obtaining abundant means for the advancement of his ambitious plans. His character was thoughtful and austere; his imagination ardent; and his delight was in religious meditation and lofty reveries.

He commenced his career of reformation in the attempt to define his own belief, and to raise himself above the gross superstition of his countrymen. In solitude and retirement he pondered the lessons he had learned in

Syria, and remembered that the ancient people of his mother were still expecting the promised Messiah. Being possessed of too strong an understanding to discover an emblem of divinity in the idol of which his grandsire and uncle were the high priests, his mind soared

"From nature up to nature's God,"

and discarded the national idolatry. By communion with himself, he recognised the existence of the Divinity as an eternal spirit, omnipotent, omniscient, and incapable of being represented by the idols of his people.

For fifteen years he devoted himself to the contemplation of this sublime thought, and meditated upon the scheme of his religion.

At length he declared to a few friends that he had a mission to perform, and that he was authorized by the Great God of the Universe to be his Apostle, and as such to be instrumental in the conversion of the world from idolatry to the worship of the only true God. His wife, his cousin Ali then only eleven years old, his slave Zaid, and Abu Bekr, an opulent citizen of Mecca, were his first converts. He was soon exiled from Mecca, and leaving that place with his little band of followers, he remained in obscurity for three years. Meanwhile his religion was gaining ground in other parts of Arabia, particularly in the city of Medina, which soon offered to receive him, and afford him protection. He accepted their offer; and no sooner did he enter their city than its citizens declared him to be their sovereign, and the Prophet of God. From this moment, he declared that his mission was to extend his religion by the sword, to destroy the temples of the infidels, to overthrow all idols, and to pursue unbelievers to the ends of the earth. "The sword," said he, "is the key of heaven and of hell: whoever falls fighting for Islam shall receive the pardon of his sins."

The once retired anchorite now became a conqueror. He headed his army in person, and marched against Mecca. While en route he won over the wily Bedawin, and ten thousand Arabs joined his army. He entered Mecca, where he established his seat of government as a temporal prince, and ambassadors flocked from every side to congratulate the new sovereign; and from this time he became the ruling prince of Arabia, having in three years subjugated the entire country. During his reign of six years, he sent out twenty-four military expeditions, nine of which he commanded in person. In 632, one hundred and fourteen thousand Mussulmans marched under his banner, upon which was inscribed their confession of faith: "No God but God, and Mohammed is his Prophet."

This remarkable man was the husband of sixteen wives, although he allowed his followers to have but four; and was the father of eight children, only one of whom lived to enjoy his fatherly care. But how different from the life of the meek and lowly Jesus, who had not

21 *

where to lay his head; who went about doing good, healing the sick, giving sight to the blind, and comfort to the distressed everywhere! He had no army to enforce his precepts; no sword but the sword of the Spirit, which was the "Word of God;" and was persecuted until his crucified body was no longer susceptible of pain. Though a despised Nazarene, his followers wished to make him a king; but, unlike Mohammed, he declined, for his kingdom was not of this world. Christ was born in a stable— Mohammed in a palace. Christ died the death of a felon—Mohammed that of a sovereign.

Having failed to discover the supposed analogy in the lives and characters of the founders of the two great religions of the world, let us examine their doctrines, and see if they be equally recommended by their intrinsic merits, and whether they deserve to be classed in the same category.

Mohammed did not attempt to introduce a new religion, for that would have aroused the prejudices of his countrymen. He professed to restore the only true and primitive faith which existed in the days of the Patriarchs and Prophets from Adam to Christ. His fundamental doctrine was the "Unity of God," which presented a broad foundation for a popular and universal religion. He ordained five daily prayers, and enjoined many ablutions well suited to Oriental life. He instituted the feast of Rhamadan, and the pilgrimage to Mecca—where one prayer he declared to be worth one hundred thousand prayers uttered elsewhere. He decreed that every man should distribute for charitable purposes the hundredth part of his possessions. His laws were adapted to the different circumstances of the people, and he so changed his religion as to suit every nation.

The Koran—of which Mohammed was the author—treats of death, the resurrection, the judgment, a future state of happiness and of torment, in a manner which greatly affects the imagination. At the end of the world, the righteous and the wicked must pass over *al-Sirat*, or the Bridge of Judgment, " which is as slender as the thread of a famished spider, and as sharp as the edge of a sword, across which the good are able to pass into Paradise, but the wicked inevitably fall into the abyss of hell — over which the bridge is suspended. While in torment they are shod with shoes of fire, obliged to drink filthy and scalding water, and have about their necks seventy thousand halters, each of which is held by seventy thousand angels, who drag him through fires and among poisonous serpents and dragons with seven heads." The Mussulman's place of punishment is divided into seven departments for different classes of delinquents; the first called Gehenna, designed for men who, though they believe, are wicked; from this purgatory, however, after a certain period of punishment for their sins, they are released and rewarded for their faith; the second, named

Padha, is for the Jews; the third, al-Hotamah, for Christians; the fourth, al-Sair, for the descendants of the wicked Saba, or Sabæans; fifth, for Magicians, or Persian Magi; sixth, al-Jahim, for idolaters; the last, and lowest, al-Hawyer, for hypocrites.

Their future place of happiness is called Jannat—a garden—corresponding to the Greek word Paradise. Its situation is above the seventh Heaven, next under the throne of God. To indicate the richness of the soil, they say it is of the finest wheat flour, musk, and saffron. It is watered, says the Koran, with streams consisting of some delightful beverage; in some places with unchangeable milk, some with clarified honey, and some with wine. But the highest delight is to be derived from the society of the Houris, or the beautiful girls with black eyes, who are formed of musk, and reside in the pavilions of hollow pearls, one of which is sixty miles long. There are eight gates to this Mohammedan Paradise, each of which leads to a different abode of happiness, graduated according to the merits of the person: the first or highest degree for the prophets; the next for the doctors and teachers of the word; the next for the martyrs; the rest for different classes according as they deserve to be blessed. The meanest inhabitant will have an extravagant number of wives and servants, and every dinner will be served up in three hundred dishes of gold.

There are many striking passages in the Mohammedan Scriptures, a few of which may not be uninteresting:—

"Do not give way to avarice; avarice is a tree which the devil hath planted in Hell, and whose branches spread over the earth. Whoever seeketh to gather its fruit is entangled in them and swept into the fire."

"Generosity is a tree planted in Heaven by God, the Lord of the world; its branches descend to the earth; man will climb up by it into paradise."

"Alms that are given in faith, without ostentation and in secret, extinguish the wrath of God, and preserve from a violent death. They quench sin as water quencheth the fire. They shut the seventy gates of evil."

"The Prophet hath said,—whosoever entereth Mecca shall issue from it like the newly-born child. The Lord looks down every night upon the earth; the first town that he seeth is Mecca: those whom he seeth first are those who kneel and pray. One hundred and twenty mercies descend daily from Heaven on Mecca: sixty for those who pray, forty for those who fast, and twenty for the lookers-on. Hell shall remove two hundred years' march, and Heaven shall draw nigh two hundred years, to the man who bears the heat of Mecca."

But enough of this. Let us turn to the sublime truths of Christianity. How gladdening to the heart, and refreshing to the soul of the Christian, is the spirit which pervades the

Bible, and how striking the contrast to every mind!

Whatever of truth is found in Mohammedanism existed already in Christianity; and the remaining doctrines of the Koran are as the dark clouds which obscure the sun, and cast a shade and gloom upon the earth. Mohammedanism recognises the God of the Jew; but so far as Christ's.claims to Divinity, and the existence of the Holy Spirit, are concerned, it is Unitarianism.

In the Mussulman's confession of faith, "There is no God but God, and Mohammed is his Prophet." Mohammed claimed a divine mission, and enforced his title by the sword, which was the most powerful logic of his religion—but Christ, who claimed to be the Son of God, established his claims by an exhibition of divine power, in the performance of well-attested miracles. He appealed not to the credulity of the people, but said, "If ye believe not me, believe me for my works' sake"—and when John the Baptist sent his friends to see if he were indeed the Christ, Jesus answered not their questions, but told them to tell John the things which they had seen, and the miracles which he had performed in their presence. Mohammed reluctantly submitted to the test of miracles; he knew too well the danger of detection in founding a religion upon miracles, which none but a God could perform.

Christ was the promised Messiah. His coming had been foretold by the prophets of ancient times. Mohammed admitted all this, and professed to be an apostle sent of God. He taught the people that their good works would procure their salvation; but our Saviour declared, " I am the way, the truth, and the life—no man cometh unto the Father but by me." The religion of Christ was one of peace and good-will to men—that of Mohammed was one of sensuality, pride, and war. While the religion of both overturned idolatry, and established the worship of the great God of the Universe,

22

Christianity was one of purity and holiness, while the other was one of superstition and gross immoralities.

The analogy which we have been seeking is found therefore only in their united opposition to idol worship. That there is, however, a great similarity in the rapid progress of both over the earth, none will deny; and the fact that there are 178,000,000 Mohammedans and 268,000,000 Christians, of whom 68,000,000 only are Protestants, is of sufficient importance to induce a careful inquiry into the method adopted by the founders of each in the propagation of their doctrines.

The policy which controlled the course of Mohammed was admirably adapted to suit the age, and the different nations in which his religion was received. Among the Jews he contended for the authority of the books of Moses; with the Christians he acknowledged the divine mission of Christ, and the truth of his gospel, and incorporated the revelations of the Old and New Testament into his own teachings. He conciliated the affections of the Arabs by showing great indulgence to their prejudices, and adding the sanction of Heaven to many of their ancient customs. We have now only to follow him to the battle-field, where he made thousands of converts, and to the Koran, in which he promises Paradise to all believers, to see how his religion made such wonderful and rapid progress. The introduction of Christianity, and the difficulties with which it contended, and over which it finally triumphed, when compared with the success of Islamism, exhibits a most striking contrast.

Christ had twelve apostles whom He commanded to go into all the world and preach His gospel to every creature. These were humble men of a despised race, and, with one exception, were ignorant and unacquainted with the logic of the schools; and the fact that they preached a new religion was not the least impediment in the way of their success. Yielding to no other system or creed, they professed to teach the only true religion. Had Christianity been content to occupy a place among other religions, without urging its claims to stand alone, it might have been tolerated. Its exclusiveness, however, was not the only novelty of this new faith; its character as a system of doctrine, and a rule of life, became a barrier in its way which human wisdom could never overcome. The languages of Greece and Rome scarcely afforded expressions by which to explain anything holy, humble, and self-denying, without the coinage of new words for the purpose. The necessity of a life of secret prayer, of faith, and a heart animated with charity and benevolence to all mankind; and, above all, a reliance upon the death and mediation of one who had been crucified as a malefactor,—for peace with God, were novelties and doctrines which were not easily comprehended by the warlike, bigoted, and self-righteous people of that age. Consequently, all the influence

of every priesthood among Jews, Gentiles, and
Pagans, opposed its progress among their disciples. These priests held the reins of public
opinion, and made a tremendous resistance to
this new religion. The authority of the magistrates was arrayed in open hostility to the Gospel, and the wisdom and pride of the heathen
philosophers were offended by its simple truths.
The Epicureans and Stoics scoffed at the teachings of Christ. They met St. Paul with taunts
and sneers—calling him a babbler and "a setter
forth of strange gods." When these doctrines
were taught, all nations were at peace, and the
minds of men were capable of giving each truth
a deliberate and a thorough investigation. It
was the Augustan age, in which the public
mind was turned towards philosophy, and
polite literature was highly cultivated. Every
man was a skeptic, and required a thorough
demonstration of every principle received. No
imposture could have remained undiscovered,
and no religion, claiming to be founded on

22 *

prophecy and miracle, could have survived the critical examination to which it would have been subjected, if it were not based upon Heaven-sanctioned truth. The murder of the meek and lowly Jesus was a great source of distress and discouragement to his followers. Their Leader had fallen, and many supposed that a death-blow had been given to their cause; and the fact that He, who claimed to be God, and to have power over death, had died in disgrace, was a heavy misfortune to those who were then obliged to labor alone under the blood-stained banner of the cross.

The mode which they adopted was not calculated to insure success. They made no compromise with the habits and the corruptions of men; they sought not the aid of secular power, and asked no favor from worldly influence, nor did they regard wealth, learning, or rank—they gloried in nothing save the Cross of Christ.

They were met everywhere by the fiercest persecutions. From the death of Christ to the fourth century of the Christian era, persecution did not cease. Stephen was stoned. James was slain with the sword. Peter and Paul were scourged, imprisoned, and persecuted continually. The ingenuity of man was exhausted in the invention of tortures for the early Christians. Some were sawn asunder—some given to wild beasts, while others were crucified and burned alive. Nations combined to crush out the disciples of Christ, and all the powers of earth and hell seemed bent on their utter extermination. If Christianity had been an invention of man, it must have utterly perished. But how did it succeed? In about six weeks from the death of Christ, His disciples began to preach, throwing their colors to the breeze where persecution commenced—in Jerusalem. Peter preached to the murderers of Christ, and three thousand souls were added to the number of Christians in one day. In a little time that number was increased to five thousand; and, in less than three years, " churches were gathered throughout all Judea, Galilee, and Samaria, and were multiplied." In seven years from the crucifixion of Christ, the Gospel was preached to the Gentiles, and with such success that churches were established in Asia Minor, Greece, Africa, and even in Italy and Rome. Tens of thousands united annually with this infant church, until their number has reached two hundred and sixty-eight millions. This great success, in the face of so many difficulties, stamps the Christian religion with the seal of God.

Mohammed began his work among the rich and great. Jesus commenced among the poor. The first three years of Mohammed were consumed in attaching to his cause thirteen of the chief people of Mecca. During the three years of Christ's ministry on earth, twelve obscure Jews were his chosen followers. The apostles of Mohammed attained to richers and honors— the command of armies and the government of kingdoms. The apostles of Christ endured the utmost poverty, scorn, and persecution, and all but one died a violent death in the defence of their Master's cause. The sixth century was propitious to the cause of Mohammed, when darkness and ignorance prevailed, and the tribes of Arabia were at war. Christianity arose in the Augustan age. The religion of Mohammed was proclaimed in an inland town of Arabia among barbarous people. The religion of Christ was preached in the most splendid city of an intelligent nation. In Arabia there was no established religion, and the cause of Mohammed was favored by the feuds and quarrels among the tribes. He was politic and conciliatory. Christ was bold and uncompromising. Mohammed labored twelve years before he had one convert outside the walls of his native city, because he then relied upon persuasion to gain his disciples. In half that time, Christianity, which was also propagated by persuasion, could number ten thousand converts in Judea, Galilee, and Samaria. At the end of twelve years, Mohammed took the sword—promised spoils to his soldiers, and the fairest captives, and the most voluptuous paradise, to the victorious army. Arabs joined his standard for the sake of plunder. The idolater had only to choose between death and conversion,—and Jews and Christians were allowed to select either the Koran, the tribute, or the sword. The success of Mohammed was that of the politician and the warrior. The success of Christ was that of a God.

The Mohammedan religion is a mixture of Judaism, Christianity, and idolatry, embellished with the fanciful imaginations of its author. Christianity is a religion of purity and love, which stands out in bold relief from the dark background of that age of impiety and sin—as a bright star shining forth from the bosom of midnight; and, when our world shall be rolled away into the graveyard of the universe, the Cross of Christ will be the emblazoned tombstone upon which shall appear the story of man's weakness and God's love.

CHAPTER XVIII.

THE JEWS.

"Jerusalem, thy prayer is heard:
His blood is on thy head!"

THERE are no people more worthy of our
attention and regard than the people of Israel,
God's own chosen race. And those inhabiting
Jerusalem claim not only our serious consideration, but most heart-felt pity. Their condition
is a sad and wonderful verification of the sure
word of prophecy, which long ago doomed
them to their present state of degradation and
woe. They are now beginning to come to Jerusalem in great numbers; and are supported
while there mainly by contributions from
abroad, amounting to the miserable pittance of
a few paras a day for each person. Yet they

are quite happy and contented, so long as they enjoy the privilege of treading the land of their forefathers, and living on the sacred soil of their beloved Mount Zion. The heart of the lover of Israel is often made to bleed when witnessing instances of the tyranny exercised over them by their despotic lords, the Turks; such as a poor old Jew being pelted with stones by the little Turkish boys in the street. The little scamps are greatly amused with the sport; and, instead of meeting with a severe rebuke, they are rewarded with encouragement from their seniors; at whose instigation, indeed, the sport is generally commenced.

No Jew is allowed to enter the Church of the Holy Sepulchre; and, indeed, should one be seen even passing through the court, he is instantly attacked by an infuriated mob of Christians, who if they allow him to escape with his life, he has great occasion to thank them, as they are fully empowered to kill him by express firman of the Sultan. He is set

GROUP OF JEWS AND JEWESSES.

free only on condition of submission to the
practice his soul abhors—of kissing a crucifix
of the despised Nazarene, or an image of the
Virgin Mary. One privilege, however, is
granted the poor Jew of Jerusalem, upon
which he places inestimable value: that of
performing his devotions close by the remains
of the magnificent walls that once surrounded
the Temple. For this favour, they at one
time paid an enormous price to the Turks,
who own not only this spot, but nearly all of
the Holy City. And there they resort at all
times, but particularly on Friday, to weep and
lament that their Temple is no more.

Here, too, assemble multitudes of the matrons
and maids of Israel, to pour forth their bitter
lamentations and scalding tears through the
crevices of that portion of the wall nearest the
site of their beloved but unapproachable Temple; "deeply wailing, deeply wailing that the
daughter of Zion is left as a cottage in a vineyard, as a lodge in a garden of cucumbers; as

23

a besieged city." But so down-trodden, impotent, and helpless are they, that it is no uncommon thing for " certain lewd fellows of the baser sort," of Turkish, Arab, and Christian pedigree, so to annoy them, that they are glad to ensconce themselves in their crowded and comfortless tenements on Mount Zion.

Fervent and many are the kisses they imprint upon these hallowed stones; and sad and plaintive are the touching words of the Karaite Jews :—

Cantor.   On account of the palace which is laid waste,
People.   We sit down alone and weep.
Cantor.   On account of the Temple which is destroyed,
People.   We sit down alone and weep.
Cantor.   On account of the walls which are pulled down,
People.   We sit down alone and weep.
Cantor.   On account of our majesty which is gone,
People.   We sit down alone and weep.
Cantor.   On account of our great men who have been cast down,
People.   We sit down alone and weep.
Cantor.   On account of the precious stones which are burned,
People.   We sit down alone and weep.

Cantor. On account of the priests who have stumbled,
People. We sit down alone and weep.
Cantor. On account of our kings who have despised him,
People. We sit down alone and weep.

SECOND CHANT.

Cantor. We beseech thee have mercy upon Zion.
People. Gather the children of Jerusalem.
Cantor. Make haste the Redeemer of Zion.
People. Speak to the heart of Jerusalem.
Cantor. May beauty and majesty surround Zion.
People. And turn with thy mercy to Jerusalem.
Cantor. Remember the shame of Zion.
People. Make new again the ruins of Jerusalem.
Cantor. May the royal government shine again over Zion.
People. Comfort those who mourn at Jerusalem.
Cantor. May joy and gladness be found upon Zion.
People. A branch shall spring forth at Jerusalem.

The Tomb of Rachel is another spot held by them in great veneration; and I envy neither the head nor the heart of the stranger who can pass from Jerusalem to Bethlehem without deviating a few hundred yards from the stony path to muse awhile, and perhaps drop a tear at the tomb of the ill-fated but " beautiful and well-favored" Rachel. The pillar set upon her grave, thirty-five long centuries and a generation ago, has long since crumbled into dust, or, more probably, been chipped into fragmentary amulets; but the venerated spot is still marked, and no doubt correctly indicated by a picturesque mausoleum, containing two rooms, the innermost of which is the consecrated sanctum where her idolized remains lie interred beneath a rude oblong tomb of plastered stones, four or five feet in height; Ephrath, or Ephratah, being but a mile or two distant; for "she was buried in the way to Ephrath, which is Bethlehem;" "and there was but a little way to go to Ephrath." Ramah, in the Hebrew, means an eminence, and it was doubtless on the top of the intervening hill in the coasts of Bethlehem, and not at Ramley, near Joppa, as Charlotte Elizabeth imagines (in that admirable production of her pen, "Judah's Lion"), that a "voice was heard"—lamentations and bitter weeping—"Rachel weeping for her children,

THE TOMB OF RACHEL.

refusing to be comforted because they were not."

How touchingly is the traveller reminded of that soul-rending cry, in passing this cherished monument of the mother of millions of the noblest race on earth — where, beneath its dome and around its walls, he hears the plaintive wailings of the daughters of this revered " mother in Israel." But they weep not for the hecatombs of innocent infants, sacrificed in the vain attempt of Herod the Great (monster of cruelty) to destroy the infant Messiah; for that event they profess to disbelieve. They are weeping for their own state of hopeless degradation, and the misery that has come upon them. Well did our adorable Redeemer say to certain devoted females, who had ministered to him of their substance, and, faithful to the bitter end, sorrowfully followed Him to Golgotha, " Weep not for me, but weep for yourselves and your children." Oh! the untold miseries that have come upon the degraded

23 *

daughter of Zion! Fountainless indeed must be the eye that can witness the harrowing anguish of mind and contortion of body manifested around this tomb, and shed no tear. Harder than the nether mill-stone, and "deaf to pity's soul-subduing cry," that bosom that can remain unmoved amid such a scene of wailing, lamentation, and despair.

Travellers have full liberty to visit the synagogues, and seldom fail to avail themselves of the privilege. But oh! how painful to witness the clamor, confusion, and utter want of solemnity with which their worship is conducted!

The women are not allowed to participate in the service, or even to sit in the body of the synagogue, but are allotted a place in the gallery, which is partitioned off by lattice work. Part of the service consists in a proclamation by a crier, who loudly proclaims the merits of the law, and offers the privilege of carrying it from the ark to the reader's stand to the highest bidder; and sometimes a large sum is given for the honor, though usually the privilege is sold for about one dollar. During the whole of their service, whether chanting or reading from the law, they continually sway their bodies to and fro. This practice they satisfactorily account for by citing one of the Psalms, where David says, "All my bones shall praise thee!"

Oh! that these walls may soon echo the glad sound of praises to Christ their true Messiah, whom they still continue to reject, to their temporal woe as well as eternal condemnation; for to this rejection may be ascribed all the evils and misery to which they are subject. How fervently should we pray that their hardness of heart may be taken away from them! for then, and not until then, are we to realize the promise that, "the fullness of the Gentiles being come in, the blindness that has happened to them in part shall be removed, and they shall be graffed into their own olive tree."

The feasts of Tabernacles, Purim, and Passover are still strictly observed. During the feast of Tabernacles, the Jewish quarter presents a very pretty and rural sight. As in olden days, booths of brush and shrubbery are erected in the courts and gardens, or on the roof of every house, and form pleasant retreats for the family. The afternoon of each day finds every household gathered in their cool and refreshing shade—some, with Talmud in hand, stand with their faces toward the Temple and chant, while those preferring a less rigid observance indulge in fruits, sherbet, and pipes.

The passover is sadly changed. Instead of killing a lamb and observing the solemn ritual of the Bible, every family slaughters a chicken, which is eaten with salt, vinegar, and herbs.

Still more absurd, and at the same time painful and disgusting, is their manner of celebrating the feast of Purim, when every Jew, both young and old, male and female, is required to become so intoxicated as to be unable

to distinguish between cursing Haman and
blessing Mordecai. How deplorable is such a
departure from the law of Moses, which indeed
is now almost entirely discarded by them!

And this is the sad but true story of the
fallen state of the house of Israel! Nor is
their temporal welfare better than their spiri-
tual. Greater wretchedness and poverty than
that in which they are sunk could not be conceived. Their quarter is the most filthy,
miserable part of the city. The hardest heart
is moved to pity on visiting their dark, closely-
packed hovels; for although their numbers are
so great, their quarter occupies but a small
portion of the city.

There are a few Karaite Jews among them,
who reject the Talmud; consequently the persecution they receive at the hands of their
talmudical brethren is very great. By way of
ineffaceably impressing this deadly hate on the
hearts of their children, they are early taught
that should they ever see a Christian and a

Karaite Jew in the act of drowning, they must overlook the Karaite and save the Christian— hateful as he is!

Should a Jew at the head of a family be- come a Christian, his wife, children, and pro- perty are taken from him, and he is in various ways bitterly persecuted, thus greatly enhanc- ing the difficulties in the way of converting them to Christianity.

What an awful lesson of unbelief and hard- ness of heart do we behold in this people, cast out, as it were, from the common rights and sympathies of all, and alienated from the in- heritance of their fathers! And how earnest should be our endeavors to convert them, see- ing that such glorious promises are predicated upon their salvation! For when the "Re- deemer shall come out of Zion, and turn away ungodliness from Jacob, all Israel shall be saved, and the gentile year of jubilee shall also arrive—for if the fall of them be the riches of the world, and the diminishing of them the riches of the gentiles, how much more their fullness? And if the casting away of them be the reconciling of the world, what shall the receiving of them be but life from the dead?"

CHAPTER XIX.

THE CHRISTIANS.

THE Christians of Jerusalem are divided into many sects—the Roman and Greek Catholics, Armenians, Copts, Syrians, and Abyssinians. Each of these sects has its separate chapel in the Church of the Holy Sepulchre, besides others scattered over the city. The "Scarlet Lady" is well represented here, as elsewhere, and has made good use of her overflowing coffers, in erecting churches and other public edifices. The Roman Catholic monks are generally the originators of the traditions with which the Holy City abounds; shall we, therefore, engage this polite old monk as our cicerone during a visit to the Church of the Holy Sepulchre, with every part of which he is no doubt familiar?

We find both the court and building thronged with pilgrims from all parts of the world, engaged in their devotional exercises. On a raised divan near the door the Turkish guards are seated, who make it their business to keep these Christians in order; and not unfrequently are their instruments of punishment brought into requisition during the festivities of Easter, when nothing is more common than a riot among the unruly multitude within. A short distance from the door is the stone of unction—a marble slab upon which Christ is said to have been laid for his anointing. A little further is a circular enclosure, marking the spot occupied by the holy women when witnessing the crucifixion. The Holy Sepulchre itself is a small building of white marble, standing beneath the dome of the church, and overhung by a star-spangled canopy. It is crowned with a cupola, and the doorway is supported by slender spiral columns. Within, the air is laden with the perfume of flowers, and the ceiling hung with

24

gold and silver lamps—the gifts of kings and princes. This too is thronged with pilgrims. Some, prostrating themselves on the floor, rub their foreheads in the dust of the pavement, while others press their lips upon the cold marble of the tomb.

We now ascend by a flight of steep steps to the scene of the crucifixion; a gaudy chapel, in which our guide points out a fissure in the rock, under the altar, caused, he tells us, by the earthquake that occurred at the death of Christ. Descending into the subterranean part of the church, we enter the chapel in which the cross was found. Here, it is said, the Empress Helena caused workmen to dig for the three crosses, which, after a diligent search, they are said to have found, and were enabled to select that on which Christ was crucified, by its miraculous powers of healing.

The Tomb of Joseph of Arimathea, is also shown. Indeed, the traditions connected with this huge pile of buildings are endless; and, soon becoming weary of these long dark corridors, gaudy chapels, and absurd traditions, we are glad once more to gain the street.

No one but an eye-witness can conceive of the scenes enacted within its walls, during the festivities of Easter. Multitudes come from distant lands to witness the gross deception and ludicrous farce played off by the Greeks, who pretend to bring down fire from heaven. This practice was originated in the following manner :—

Many years ago, a devout bishop, on making his accustomed examination of the lamps of the Church of the Sepulchre, prior to the Easter ceremonies, found that every drop of oil had been exhausted; he filled them with water, and prayed that success might attend the experiment. After earnestly putting up his petition, he was rewarded by seeing the church flooded with light—fire having descended from Heaven and miraculously ignited the water. This encouraged him to repeat the experiment, which his successors have continued to perform, on every recurrence of Easter, to the present day. They extinguish all the lights, and then conceal themselves within the sepulchre, having first supplied themselves with matches and alcohol. Meantime the expectant people are impatient to behold the wonderful miracle, which they firmly believe is about to transpire. While in waiting, there is anything but order preserved—they crawl on the floor —pray loudly for the descent of the fire, and mount one another's shoulders—forming moving pyramids of human beings. Meanwhile, the emissaries of the false prophet lustily apply the whip on all sides, but without the desired effect; men run and jump, and gallop to and fro, through the church. To increase the attractions of the juggling show, some are dressed in Jewish costume, and these are treated with a mock display of anger. The multitude unite in heaping upon them all manner of insult, and drive them through the church with derisive shouts of laughter, to show the low repute in which they are held. A procession is now formed of priests and bishops, bearing crucifixes, torches, and other paraphernalia. They halt before every image, picture, and flower-adorned altar, to beseech the aid of Heaven in the miracle. The announcement being made that the multitude may soon expect the appearance of the heavenly flame, all eyes are directed to the circular windows of the sepulchre; and now, from one of them, the fire is seen to issue forth. A sudden rush is made, and, not unfrequently, some are killed, and many wounded, in the struggle of the mighty mass to reach the flame. Some apply it to their beards, hands, and faces, while others burn the edges of the linen intended for their burial clothes. By means of a cord, even those in the gallery succeed in lighting their tapers. Those not as successful as others knock down their more fortunate brethren, and, by force, deprive them of their torches. The bishops,

24 *

who were concealed in the sepulchre, now leave their hiding-place, and are borne aloft by the crowd with frantic shouts of joy.

How hideous the spectacle that reigns throughout the building—the air dense with the smoke of thousands of burning tapers—the people furiously rushing to and fro, each one loudly shouting and giving thanks in his own language, and the whips of the Turkish soldiers in full performance of the duties of their office!

A shout is heard from the court! It is the imperious demand of the Bethlehemites for admission. They have been despatched by the Patriarch on the fleetest horses his stable affords, to obtain some of the holy fire, with which to light the lamps of the Church of the Nativity.

The more enlightened portion of the Greek church acknowledge that this famous miracle is all a hoax; but, then, to confess this openly, would greatly endanger the craft of the priests.

Well may the poor deluding priest say with
Macbeth :—

> " I am in blood
> Stept in so far, that, should I wade no more,
> Returning were as tedious as go o'er."

At another time, during holy week, a scene
equally painful and revolting occurs, when the
service of the crucifixion is enacted by the
Roman Catholics—other sects taking no part
in the performance, except by doing all they
possibly can, to annoy them. The Franciscan
monks commence the ceremonies by forming
a procession, and making the circuit of the
church, chanting the " *Miserère*," and wafting
incense before each altar. The wax figure,
representing the Saviour, is taken down from
the cross, and the nails extracted from the
hands and feet, while the people gather
around it and weep. Having wrapped it in
a linen sheet, it is laid on the slab of unction
and anointed. Many discourses being deli-
vered, and the body taken the grand rounds

of the church, it is sprinkled with rose water, and carried to the sepulchre, there to remain until Easter, when another mockery will be performed called the service of the resurrection.

Such are the unhallowed scenes presented to the eyes of the Jews and Mohammedans by the so-called Christians. Such being the exhibition of Christianity in Jerusalem, no wonder that the unbelieving Jew, and scoffing Mohammedan, still continue in their obstinate rejection of Christ! Oh, that this city may soon be fully supplied with true missionaries of the Cross, who will faithfully exhibit the Gospel both in their lives and teachings!

CHAPTER XX.

FRUITS OF PALESTINE.

"Blossoms, and fruits, and flowers, together rise,
And the whole year in gay confusion lies."

THE country around Jerusalem affords a great diversity of climate and soil, and therefore many varieties of fruits. Immediately around the city, hoarfrosts, if known at all, are very slight, and touch but lightly either fruits or vegetables; and water seldom freezes even in midwinter. During the summer, cool breezes are enjoyed almost throughout the day, varied occasionally by the hot, oppressive sirocco, which blows from the parched sands of the desert. Such is the mildness of the winter, that oranges, dates, figs, pomegranates, lemons, apricots, almonds, and grapes grow throughout the season, requiring no protection whatever.

A curious anecdote is connected with a plant peculiarly Oriental—the mandrake. The fragrance of its berries tempted a Scotch sojourner in the Holy City, to try it as an edible. The root was subjected to a long process of boiling, stewing, and frying, and then our prying friend proceeded to satisfy his curiosity and appetite, little imagining its wondrous effects. The night of the experiment was passed in the agony of fear and frightful dreams. On awaking in the morning, he fancied he was surrounded by snakes; and conceiving his watch chain to be a venomous reptile, he actually bit the precious metal in pieces. Every straw, string, and thread he imagined were reptiles, and dropped them in alcohol for preservation. The tables and chairs, which he conceived to be robbers, were found broken into fragments.

He presented a most hideous spectacle, being sadly bruised and battered in his struggles with the supposed robbers; and his eyes had a most unearthly appearance from the peculiar effects of the plant. His physicians did not readily succeed in curing him; and I dare say our unfortunate friend will not soon forget his adventure. It is an ascertained fact that no snake can approach this plant with impunity. It is doubtless on account of such remarkable properties that the Arabs term it Tufah-el-Shatan—"Apples of Satan."

A little beyond Bethlehem are the Gardens of Solomon, so beautifully alluded to in the Canticles. In this lovely spot, the most capricious taste could not complain, so varied and luscious are its fruits. The gardens are enclosed by steep and rugged mountains, whose sides abound in apricots, peaches, oranges, lemons, pomegranates, grapes, and figs. In all the flora of Syria, I know of no plant more curious (unless, indeed, the "resurrection flower" be so esteemed) than a quite weed-like plant abounding here, which bears no less than five or six different kinds of flowers. And this valley has been made more attractive still by the improvements of a party of estimable Americans, who left home and friends to cultivate the soil of Palestine, and benefit the Jews, towards whom they very substantially evince a burning zeal for their welfare.

But few palm trees remain, either in or around Jerusalem, though in other Oriental cities they are very abundant. And while enjoying their shade, and meditating upon the dispersion of the Jews, we are often reminded of a stanza from the pen of an English poet:—

> "More blest each palm that shades these plains
>   Than Israel's scattered race;
>   For, taking root, it there remains
>   In solitary grace:
>   It cannot quit its place of birth;
>   It will not live in other earth."

Mount Olivet is planted with olive, fig,

pomegranate, mulberry,* and almond trees. Olives are eaten either pickled or soaked in olive oil. The most common dish of the Arabs, is an earthen vessel of olives, and a loaf of taboon bread, with which they seat themselves under the shade of a tree, seeming to be perfectly contented with their simple fare. Their bread is always made flat and thin, and being not unlike leather in respect to toughness and pliability, they easily mould it into the shape of a spoon, with which they dip up the olives, rice, or whatever they may be eating. Their hands, however, are used quite as often as the spoon of taboon bread, and thought to be much the more convenient of the two.

So abundant are oranges and lemons, that twenty oranges can be bought for a piastre,

* I may be allowed to mention, for the benefit of whom it may concern, a fact I learned of the Arabs, when I had one day accidentally stained my dress with mulberry juice,—that is, that the leaf if bruised on the stain will effectually remove it.

and thirty lemons for the same small sum. Citrons abound in almost as great profusion.

The karub tree is sometimes to be met with, the pods of which are said to have been the food of the prodigal son. The word "husk" used in the New Testament, correctly translated, would be "little horn," which exactly coincides in shape with these pods. It is still used in some parts of the world for feeding swine, but in Syria it is in great requisition with the poorer class, who use it as their daily food.

The cactus or prickly pear grows to an immense size, and bears a most palatable, juicy fruit. It is also formed into hedges for vineyards, gardens, and paths; perhaps it was to the latter that the Saviour referred in the parable of the supper: "Go out into the highways and hedges, and compel them to come in." We may also infer that this secure and thorny hedge is referred to in Mark—"A certain man planted a vineyard, and set an hedge about it."

In addition to the fruits already mentioned, pears and bananas are raised. Grapes are in season during five months of the year, and are converted into unadulterated wine by the Jews and Christians, and raisins by the Mohammedans, wine being forbidden them by their *temperate* prophet. Indeed, the Syrian climate produces almost every variety of fruit, grain, and vegetables to be found in our western soil, the American colonists having eminently succeeded in the cultivation of every article introduced by them except the apple.

If we visit the market in October, the streets will be found lined with baskets of olives, grapes, pistachio nuts, radishes, lettuce, and other vegetables of rapid growth. In November, the olives and grapes being scarce, they bring dates instead. The juice of the grapes is converted into molasses, called by them " dibis." Grapes are also converted into raisins, which, together with figs, are placed in the still for the formation of arrack, the Oriental alcohol. In

December, when the country no longer wears
a barren aspect, but is covered with richest
verdure, cabbages, cauliflowers, radishes, lettuce,
and lentiles are brought to the city. After
January, corn is no longer brought to market;
but we can well dispense with it now, for we
have in Syria three crops a year. This is the
month in which the almond, apricot, peach,
and plum trees are clothed with their rich and
fragrant blossoms. Oranges, lemons, citrons,
and limes are brought in great abundance. In
February the bazaars are lined with flowers,
hyacinths, daffodils, tulips, ranunculuses, lilies,
narcissus, geraniums, scarlet poppies, ane-
mones, and daisies. Most of the vegetables
and fruits already named are still in great
abundance, with the addition of onions, carrots,
and beets; and in March, beans, sage, thyme,
and mint are added; and now the pear, black
thorn, fig, palm, and apple trees bloom, while
orange and lemon trees are still heavily laden
with fruit and flowers. To these may be added

celery, parsley, and other herbs. In April,
vegetation being very abundant, the list becomes longer : white mulberry, artichokes,
peas, beans, onions, cucumbers, lettuce, corn,
the Arab potato, and a vegetable something
like the turnip, lavender, rosemary, and the
supposed rose of Sharon. In May, cucumbers,
tomatoes, onions, potatoes, corn, a small species
of apple, and late in the month, muskmelons,
watermelons, cantelopes, walnuts, blackberries,
and the mulberry fig. In June there is an
abundance of cherries, figs, plums, damascenes,
quinces, olives, almonds, bananas, pomegranates,
plantains, grapes, egg-plant, licorice root, dan-
delion, and henna. In July, peaches, grapes,
pears, nectarines, melons, plums, potatoes, egg-
plant, prickly pear, Indian fig, pumpkins, dates,
damascenes. In August a still greater variety
of fruits and vegetables are displayed; but in
September there is a slight decrease. In this
month cotton and hemp rapidly mature, and
the Arab corn, doura, millet, and castor oil

25 *

plant, which here grows to a tree; the Egyptian maize is also brought to market. But this is by no means a complete list of the varieties of fruits, vegetables, medicinal plants, and flowers in the bazaars at different seasons of the year. The variety is almost endless; indeed, so abundant are vegetables, that but little meat is consumed, both from choice and necessity; for the only animal food to be obtained, besides fowls, is mutton and goat-meat.

CHAPTER XXI.

AN APPEAL IN BEHALF OF ORIENTAL FEMALES.

"Night wraps the realm where Jesus woke,
　　No guiding star the magi see,
　And heavy hangs oppression's yoke,
　　Where first the gospel said, 'Be free.'"

JUSTLY as America is renowned for her libe-
ral principles as "the land of the free and the
home of the brave"—the great theatre of noble
and virtuous actions, and the very pavilion of
arts, science, and literature—it is yet more
justly celebrated as the arena on which woman
is allowed the freest exercise of all the functions of her exalted mission. It is but too evident, however, that we do not either prize or
improve these rare privileges as we should.
And it has occurred to my mind that a few

words from one who has spent some years in
the East, under circumstances enabling her to
form a correct estimate of woman's character
and condition there, might not only excite in
them a deeper sense of gratitude to " Him who
hath made *us* to differ," but might also prompt
them to efforts for the amelioration of their
degraded state.

In no country is woman appreciated as she
is in blessed America—no, not in Albion's
favored isle, nor in " La Belle France," nor in
sunny Italy, nor in any place that it has been
my lot to visit, as in this happy land—Columbia Felix!

Whatever I may say upon the condition of
Oriental females, relates to those inhabiting
the once favored land of Sarah and the Marys,
the land of Esther's people, and of Ruth's
choice, of Judith, and of Phebe. Nor shall I
speak of extreme cases, but give a fair repre-
sentation of the matter just as it is, for that
truly were enough to move a heart of adamant.

GROUP OF PEASANT WOMEN.

Travellers inform us that their condition is still worse in a few other countries, but, if so, Heaven pity the poor creatures! Crown of creation, how thou art fallen, art fallen!

In no city on earth, perhaps, is woman found in greater variety than in the "City of the Great King." The fair ruby-lipped Circassian and the sable daughter of Ham, the fur-clad Russian and the semi-nude Bedawy of the desert, the graceful Greek and the clumsy Copt, the modest Armenian and the brazen Fellahah, the haughty inmate of the hareem and the oppressed Jewess, "from every nation under heaven." But, however widely they all may differ in blood, manners, customs, and appearance; they all more or less resemble each other in at least this common point—they are the abject slaves of the "lords of creation." If then you would form a proper estimate of the lot and condition of woman in her Oriental phases, you need not go beyond the precincts of Jerusalem. Do you see that white sheet and thick veil, enveloping something, whose yellow boots suggest the idea that it may be a piece of living humanity? Shade of Eve, it is a daughter of yours! Reader, it is a sister of ours! Those black slaves are sent to hold her in vile surveillance. The lordly Effendi, the bigoted church dignitary, the panoplied soldier, and the proud civilian, all pass her without the slightest salutation, though they well know from her train that she is as respectable as a woman can be in the East. Nay, her own brother vouchsafes not the slightest token of recognition, even averting his head as he passes; and were her own husband to condescend to exchange a few words with her in public, he would be considered not only as utterly disgraced, but as having actually sinned. Cruel Turk, who

> " Scorns the world,
> And struts about with whiskers curled,
> Keeps a thousand wives under lock and key,
> For nobody else but himself to see."

He says he has bought her, and will treat her as he pleases! But, probably you think that domestic happiness within doors may somehow or other compensate for the neglect with which she is treated in public. Ah! you have little conception of woman's sad condition throughout the Orient! Never can you say of an Oriental dwelling, as the poet has of an English cottage—

"I knew by the smoke, that so gracefully curled
    Above the tree tops, that a cottage was near,
  And I said to myself if there's peace in this world,
    The soul that is humble might hope for it there."

· There is no peace in the hareem. And what love can the monstrous tyrant have for one of them when his modicum of affection is divided amongst half a dozen or half a score, or a score and a half of poor ignorant creatures? What heart-rending scenes is the sojourner in the East continually compelled to witness, flowing from the abominations of the hareem system! Yet the instance cited is the very brightest picture of Oriental female life which can be portrayed. For these poor creatures' husband, if indeed *he* can be called *husband*, whose conjugal affection is divided amongst so many, or rather bestowed upon none, is able to support his ample household without requiring any labor at their hands.

But how widely different is the case when they are compelled to labor for their own support and his! Take another illustration then—one from the lower walks of life. You see that one-robed woman, with tattooed face and narrow little bead-adorned veil, concealing nose, mouth, and chin, while most of her person is as much exposed as Grecian sculptor could desire;—she truly has a hard lot. She is bringing vegetables to market. *She* planted the seed; *she* worked the ground; *she* gathered the crop, and now *she* must make sale of them, or else what is to become of that little fellow that rides astride her shoulder, and the babe that swings in the knapsack that hangs on her back? For her brutal husband spends the livelong day lounging in the idle group at the gathering-place of the village. Besides her own heavy cargo, she drives the donkey before her to the city, well loaded with the produce of her own industry. But does she venture to ride him back? Not she! 'Twould cost her a sound drubbing to do so. But you see her lord and master seated upon him leisurely smoking his pipe, while his help-meet carries two children and a basket.

Ladies, sympathize with your sister, for you borrow from her the present style of flowing sleeve, which you admire so much; but you do not "go the whole figure," for you will discard in a few weeks more what has been worn in the East for perhaps three thousand years. She wears it three or four times the length of yours, and either ties it around her neck, or covers her uncombed head with these useful append-ages, and they thus serve the quadruple pur-

26

poses of sleeve, cape, bonnet, and handkerchief.
But alas, poor thing, while she may wear that
robe like—

> "Beauties by Sir Peter Lelie,
> Whose drapery hints you may admire them freely,"

suppose she were so unfortunate as to be caught
without that nose-and-mouth-hiding veil,—such
shameful *immodesty* would in all probability
call down, not only the bitterest ire of her
devoted husband, and the reproaches of the
neighborhood, but a sound drubbing besides.
In what durance vile are we bound, by custom
on the one hand, and impelled by fashion on
the other! But query,—which is worse, to be
wedded to such a brute, or to fashion? Who
can say which is the more tyrannical, arbitrary,
and capricious?

Now if such are the civil and social disabili-
ties of woman in the East, how much more the
mental and moral servitude under which she
groans and toils, despairs and dies! Should we

not, henceforth, evince more gratitude to the "Author and Giver of all good," than we ever yet have done, for the distinguishing privileges we enjoy in this western world; and not only so, but, in view of our great responsibility, should we not give proof of our gratitude, by extending relief to our less favored sisters in Eastern climes?

> "Then aid with prayer that holy light
> Which from eternal death can save,
> And bid Christ's heralds speed their flight
> Ere millions find a hopeless grave."

THE END.

READY IN JULY, 1858.

Palestine, Past and Present.

BY REV. HENRY S. OSBORN, A. M.

THIS work is the result of recent researches in Palestine and a portion of Syria. It embraces the NATURAL, SCIENTIFIC, CLASSICAL, AND HISTORICAL FEATURES of this, the most interesting of all lands, and identifies and illustrates many Scriptural passages hitherto unnoticed.

It will be Illustrated by Engravings from NEW AND ORIGINAL DESIGNS, executed in the highest style of art. The Publishers will spare no expense in their department of the work. The Engravings will consist of a PANORAMIC SERIES OF ORIGINAL VIEWS, taken by the Author from the most favorable positions; giving to the Reader a perfect conception of the Cities, Villages, Architecture of the Country, and Landscape Scenery of the East. Also, Engravings of birds, flowers, ancient coins, the geological strata—comprising its fossils, minerals, &c. ; with the costumes, positions, and peculiarities of the people. The Illustrations will consist of splendid Chromographs (printed in ten rich oil colors), Tinted Lithographs, and the finest Wood Engravings.

A NEW MAP OF PALESTINE, by the Author, from actual surveys, and differing essentially from any that has yet appeared, will accompany the work.

The Literary Department will embrace scientific and critical examinations of facts as associated with the scenes presented, with a view to the elucidation of disputed points of Scripture. Also, personal observations made during a sojourn in the East; giving social, religious, and political incidents, just as they occur among all classes. An invaluable amount of information will thus be concentrated into the most perfectly illustrated work on the subject extant.

This work will be a valuable companion to "THE CITY OF THE GREAT KING;" as the Author will devote special attention to the *Land of Palestine;* referring the reader to Dr. Barclay's work for full information in reference to the Holy City.

The Views will be truthful and accurate, and will not be transfers from other works, nor libellous caricatures of Sacred Localities, as at present abound in nearly every work on the subject.

Prices :—Cloth, $3.50. Philadelphia Library, $4.00. Half-calf Antique, $4.50. Turkey, full gilt, $5.00. Super Turkey or Antique, $5.50. By mail, post paid.

Heavy discount to Agents and the Trade.

JAMES CHALLEN & SONS, Publishers,
Philadelphia, Pa.

𝔗𝔥𝔢 𝔠𝔦𝔱𝔶 𝔬𝔣 𝔱𝔥𝔢 𝔊𝔯𝔢𝔞𝔱 𝔎𝔦𝔫𝔤;

O R,

JERUSALEM AS IT WAS, AS IT IS, AND AS IT IS TO BE.

By Dr. J. T. BARCLAY, Missionary to Palestine.

627 Royal 8vo. pages, and Seventy splendid Engravings.

THIS is undoubtedly the most complete and valuable work on the Holy City ever issued. Five large editions were sold within three months of its publication, and the demand for it is increasing.

Extracts from Notices in Reviews of the Highest Authority.

Its profuse Engravings on wood, stone, and steel, leave nothing to be desired in the matter of Pictorial Embellishment. The mechanical execution of the work corresponds to the importance of the theme, and to the scientific thoroughness with which the Author has fulfilled his task.—*North American Review.*

It gives a valuable compendium of ancient and modern authorities concerning Jerusalem; a minute array of the points of its topography, drawn from the Scriptures and Josephus; careful observations upon its climate and its vital and economical statistics; valuable measurements of ancient remains; *the most accurate and reliable account of Modern Jerusalem yet given in the English language;* while, in its minute descriptions of the Water Resources of the City, of the discovery of the Great Quarry, of the interior of the Mosk of Omar, and the substructures of El-Aksa, and also the Arch of the Tyropœon Bridge, it adds not a little of substantial value to our knowledge.—*Bibliotheca Sacra.*

The volume is a magnificent one.—*Southern Baptist Review.*

It would be difficult to name any point interesting to the Biblical scholar or general reader which is not fully treated.—*Boston Quarterly Journal.*

No expense has been spared to make the work a standard work—not merely a book of pleasant reading, but for permanent value.—*Christian Examiner.*

A work of no ordinary interest.—*The Churchman.*

It is emphatically the work of the season. With the exception of the "Explorations of Dr. Kane," and the "Travels of Dr. Livingstone," no recent issue from the press has commanded equal sale.—*Presbyterian Quarterly Review.*

A most important addition to the knowledge of the present day.—*Presbyterian Magazine.*

A book of surpassing interest, and of great value to Biblical students.—*New York Commercial Advertiser.*

Not only is it rich in matter, but rich in its "getting up."—*Ladies' Repository.*

"The City of the Great King" is richly adorned with Pictorial Illustrations, many of which have been prepared at great pains and expense, and impart assurance that our publishers are gaining rapidly a position alongside of their eminent fellow-craftsmen in England.—*Boston Watchman & Reflector.*

The most important contribution ever furnished in this particular department of sacred learning.—*Colonization Herald.*

From this time, this work will rank as authority upon all matters upon which it is devoted.—*Newark Advertiser.*

Price, cloth, $3.50. Half calf, $4.50. Morocco, full gilt, $5.00. Super Turkey or Antique, $6.00. By mail, post paid.

JAMES CHALLEN & SONS, Publishers,
Philadelphia, Pa.

JAMES CHALLEN & SONS' PUBLICATIONS,

PHILADELPHIA.

THE CITY OF THE GREAT KING. Cloth, $3.50; half calf, $4.50; Turkey, gilt, $5.00; super Turkey antique, $6.00.

CARPENTRY MADE EASY. 40 plates, $3.00.

NEW JUVENILE LIBRARY. 10 vols., $2.50.

THE CAVE OF MACHPELAH, and Other Poems. Cloth, $1.00; cloth, full gilt, $1.50; morocco, full gilt, $2.00.

THE GOSPEL AND ITS ELEMENTS. Cloth, 30 cents; paper, 20 cents.

CHRISTIAN EVIDENCES. Cloth, 30 cents; paper, 20 cents.

UNION OF CHRISTIANS, AND DEATH OF CHRIST. Cloth, 40 cents; paper, 30 cents.

MAP OF JERUSALEM. By Dr. J. T. Barclay. Plain, 50 cents; colored, 75 cents; book form, $1.00; mounted, $1.75.

GRANDFIELD'S PATRIARCHAL CHAIN OF THE BIBLE. Sheet, 75 cents; mounted, $2.00.

HADJI IN SYRIA. By Sarah Barclay Johnson. Cloth, 75 cents; blue and gold, $1.00.

LADIES' CHRISTIAN ANNUAL. Cloth, gilt, 6 vols., $1.50 per vol., or $6.00 per set.

IN PRESS.

PALESTINE, PAST AND PRESENT. Cloth, $3.50; half calf, $4.50; Turkey, gilt, $5.00; super Turkey antique, $6.00.

IGDRASIL; OR, THE TREE OF EXISTENCE, and Other Poems. Cloth, 75 cents; blue and gold, $1.00.

JUVENILE LIBRARY. 20 vols., $4.00.

☞ Other Works now in course of preparation will be duly announced.

Address

JAMES CHALLEN & SONS, Publishers,
Philadelphia, Pa.

SUNDAY SCHOOL LIBRARIES, ETC.

CHRISTIAN SUNDAY SCHOOL LIBRARY.

50 vols., $8.00. This Library was edited by D. S. Burnett.

NEW JUVENILE LIBRARY FOR THE SUNDAY SCHOOL AND FAMILY.

Edited and revised by James Challen. Engravings executed in the highest style of art and printed on tinted paper.

TITLES OF SERIES NO. 1.

1. Song without Words, 25 cts.; 2. Look Up; or, Girls and Flowers, 25 cts.; 3. Home Life, 25 cts.; 4. Isabel; or, Influence, 25 cts.; 5. The Arab, 25 cts; 6. The Egyptian, 25 cts.; 7. The Jew, 25 cts.; 8. Garnered Thoughts, 25 cts.; 9. Wings and Stings, 25 cts.; 10. The Young Cottager, 25 cts.

Put up in neat boxes, $2.50.

Both the above Libraries will be sent by express for $10.

NEW JUVENILE LIBRARY.—(In Press.)

20 vols. uniform with the above, $4.00.

These works are original, by the best writers; and, as nothing sectarian is admitted, they are adapted to Sunday Schools of every denomination. Superintendents and others are requested to send in their orders now, accompanied by the price.

We also publish Dr. Barclay's MAP OF JERUSALEM and ENVIRONS, and GRANDFIELD'S PATRIARCHAL CHAIN OF THE BIBLE—both valuable for Sunday School Illustration. Price of each, mounted, colored, and varnished, (by express only,) $1.75.

Also, THE CITY OF THE GREAT KING, by Dr. J. T. Barclay, the most superb and valuable work on Jerusalem ever issued. Every Superintendent should possess a copy. Price $3.50, post paid.

HADJI IN SYRIA, by Mrs. Sarah Barclay Johnson, for three years a resident in Palestine. Over 300 pages, and 12 splendid Engravings. Price (cloth), 75 cents. Blue and gold, $1.00, by mail, post paid.

☞ This work is admirably adapted as a gift-book for children.

Sunday School Libraries selected with great care, and forwarded to any part of the Union. If Superintendents or Librarians will send us *a list of the books they have*, and a general description of the books they want, we will make judicious selections for them to any amount they may forward. The Publications of the SUNDAY SCHOOL UNION, BAPTIST PUBLICATION SOCIETY, the AMERICAN TRACT SOCIETY, and those of private publishers, will be sold on the same terms as at their respective depositories.

We also supply Sunday Schools with BIBLES, TESTAMENTS, ROLL and CLASS BOOKS. MAPS, CHARTS, &c., at the very lowest rates.

All orders will be promptly filled the day they are received.

Address

JAMES CHALLEN & SONS, Publishers,
Philadelphia, Pa.

www.ingramcontent.com/pod-product-compliance
Lightning Source LLC
LaVergne TN
LVHW051252080426
835509LV00020B/2941